CLASSIC

TEX-MEX

AND TEXAS

COOKING

AUTHENTIC RECIPES
WITH BIG, BOLD FLAVORS

Sheryn R. Jones
Cookbook Resources, LLC

Classic Tex-Mex and Texas Cooking
Authentic Recipes with Big, Bold Flavors

1ˢᵗ Printing - February 2005
2ⁿᵈ Printing - November 2005
3ʳᵈ Printing - April 2006
4ᵗʰ Printing - November 2007

International Standard Book No. 978-1-931294-63-8

Library of Congress No. 2004103878

Library of Congress Catalog Data
    Main Title: Classic Tex-Mex and Texas Cooking : Authentic Recipes with Big, Bold Flavors /
        Sheryn R. Jones.
    Description: 317 p. : ill. ; 24 cm.
    Notes: Includes index.
    Subjects: 1. Mexican American cookery. 2. Cookery, American–Southwestern style.
    TX715.2.S69 J68 2004
    641.5972 22

Illustrations by Nancy Murphy Griffith

Edited, Designed and Published in the United States of America
and Manufactured in China by
Cookbook Resources, LLC
541 Doubletree Drive
Highland Village, Texas 75077
Toll free 866-229-2665

www.cookbookresources.com

Your Ultimate Source for Easy Cookbooks

CONTENTS

 *Editor's Choice Recipes*

Texas Facts:

There are no exaggerations, idle boasts or obnoxious statements in this cookbook, only unadorned truth.

CONTENTS

 Tex-Mex Favorites
& Legendary Recipes

Slim's Tidbit:
Texas expressions and wisdom-isms

TEX-MEX AND TEXAS COOKING EXPLAINED

Every Texan would explain **Tex-Mex Food and Texas Cooking** differently, some more extensively and fervently than others, but there is no doubt that if you asked a Texan, *"What is Tex-Mex Food?"*, you would get an answer. This cookbook and this introduction are heroic, however feeble, attempts to give you an answer for what is arguably the most colorful, flavorful and indigenous regional cuisine in America and probablythe world.

There is no doubt that the explanation would be one thing in East Texas, another thing in West Texas and something different in South Texas. In fact, if you were to drive from San Antonio to Austin to Dallas on Interstate 35 and stop to eat enchiladas in all three cities as I have many times, you would find that the enchiladas are different in San Antonio, Austin and Dallas. And even though the enchiladas in all three cities are different, there is no argument that they are all definitely Tex-Mex. So, how does one explain the similarities and the differences and come up with a definition of **Tex-Mex Food** and an explanation of **Texas Cooking**?

The answer, I believe, comes in the form of exaggeration (so common among Texans) and over-simplification (also common among Texans). For instance, in Texas:

Anything with jalapeno in it or with it is Tex-Mex.

Anything that is chicken-fried is Texas Cooking. And the basic food groups in Texas are chili, barbecue, beans, jalapenos and "Meskun" food.

To add some humor to this exaggeration and over-simplification, Texas expressions and wisdom-isms are used in an effort to convey a "flavor" of the place and the people. It reminds me of the ol' boy who told me "a hundred years ago, we as sa pore, some days we as eatin chickens and some days we as eatin feathers."

And when it all comes down to *"What is Tex-Mex and Texas Cooking?"*, it reminds me of the eloquent Texan who said, "I can explain it to you. I just can't understand it for you."

And there you have it… the Texas truth of it all. After reading 320 pages of this cookbook, I'm sure you're going to know what Texas Cooking is all about. "Now, am I right or Amarillo?"

THE ORIGIN OF TEX-MEX FOOD

I guess you'd have to say that Tex-Mex Food (It's hard to call it cuisine.) really comes from cattle drives and Old Mexico, from ranchers and cowhands, from vaqueros and senoras, from mothers, grandmothers, chuck wagon cooks and from parts known and unknown.

The indigenous foods of Texas came from what was available and were fixed (cooked) the best way they could. These foods give us a glimpse into the past and the rugged independence, resourcefulness and perseverance found in Texas.

The indigenous foods of Texas are as colorful and memorable as the state's history and the characters who call themselves Texans. The flavors are big and bold, honest and simple, exotic and exciting and always memorable.

MEXICAN FOOD IN TEXAS

"Mexican food was not created by chefs with pampered palates in fine kitchens. Instead, it was improvised by people with simple cooking facilities who used what foods were available. Juan Almonte in his statistical report on Texas in 1835 stated that, 'the food most generally used among Mexicans in Texas is tortilla, beef, venison, chickens, eggs, cheese and milk; sometimes, bread, chocolate, tea and sugar.' Frequently, however, it was necessary for a family to subsist on nothing more than beans and tortillas.

"In former days tortillas were made by soaking shelled corn in lime water overnight or until the husks soften. The corn was then ground on a stone metate with a bit of lime water, producing a paste called masa. A small pinch of the masa was patted between the cook's hands and then pressed paper thin. Some lime water was evaporated on the comal, a flat griddle with a fire below it, before the tortillas were placed on it to cook. Each tortilla was browned on both sides before serving. Today, however, few individuals make their own tortillas in Texas, because they are made in most grocery stores and tortillerias...

"The regional foods of Texas-Mexicans differ from the traditional dishes of Mexico and the ingredients vary with individual tastes. All, however, are generally hearty, filling and highly seasoned. Among the most common seasonings are peppers of various types, comino (cumin), coriander, cilantro, onions and garlic."

The Melting Pot: Ethnic Cuisine in Texas
Published by The Institute of Texan Cultures of The University of Texas at San Antonio

ODE TO BAR B QUE

Ain't had much luck with horses,
Last 'un stomped my head.
Ain't had much luck with women,
Last 'un wished me dead.

Ain't had much luck with lots of things,
But this I'll tell you true.
There is one thing I've got luck with;
It's Texas Bar B Que.

Bar-B-Que's as old as time;
The caveman smoked a bit.
He could've won the Bedrock Fair,
If he'd just had my kit.

A dirt hole or a metal pit.
Watch closely while it makes.
You'll get a good scald on them ribs,
If you've got what it takes.

A hickory fire of seasoned wood---
A secret old folks knew.
Smoked until the char is right,
It ain't no brie fondue.

The brisket stands without the sauce;
This ain't no French filet.
That meat's a'fallin' off the bone;
You've cooked the "Lone Star" way."

Don't worry none 'bout horses' feet,
Or fret 'bout opposite sexes.
Get a pit and fire it up
BAR-B-QUE---DONE BEST IN TEXAS!

~Lanny Joe Burnett

Cowboy Poet Lanny Joe Burnett was raised on a ranch in Fannin County, Texas. The son of fourth generation Texans, Lanny has been a cowboy all his life. He has performed at the Red Steagall Cowboy Gathering in Fort Worth, the Texas Cowboy Reunion in Stanford, National Cowboy Symposium in Lubbock, State Fair of Texas in Dallas, Fort Worth Stock Show in Fort Worth, Monterey Cowboy Gathering in Monterey, California, in Europe, Central Asia and in many gatherings, festivals, story-telling meetings, churches, schools and benefits across Texas and the American Southwest.

SLIM'S TIDBITS

Slim was a trail-ridin, slop-slingin', older than black pepper, cowboy chuck wagon cook. To use my Daddy's way of describing somebody, "He's a long, tall drink of water, and he minds his own biscuits (stays out of other people's business). He's a good guy. If he likes you, he'll give you his last biscuit if he can have half of it. If he doesn't like you, he'll cloud up and rain all over you. But, he's honest, straight-forward and he'll tell you the Texas truth of it."

While most people in Texas do not talk like Slim, he is part of our legacy. And it is up to each of us to continue the exaggerations, boastful claims and colorful language that together make Texas the biggest place in the world. Hope you enjoy some of Slim's funnin'.

Slim's Tidbit:
Texas expressions and wisdom-isms

Editor's Choice Recipes
The Editor's Choice Recipes
are some of the editor's favorites

Tex-Mex Favorites & Legendary Recipes
Tex-Mex Favorites and Legendary Recipes
are recipes most Texans grow up eating.

Texas facts and unadorned truths. It is what it is.

TEXAS AND TEX-MEX DICTIONARY

Armadillo-Road bump

Back burner-Where you put something when you don't want to do it

Barbecue-Beef brisket; not a verb or adjective; not a noun meaning equipment; barbecue is brisket

Bet 'chur boots-A sure thing; definitely

Bowl of Red-Chili; meat dish with no beans

Boy howdy!-Affirmative; exclamatory comment; "Boy howdy, that was good!"

Boy, I mean!-Affirmative

Branch-Usually means water; J.R. drank bourbon and branch

Brisket-Barbecue

Buck fever-Gets too excited; blows it; refers specifically to missing a shot while deer hunting; "He's got buck fever sa bad, he thought that tree had horns."

Burrito -Warmed soft flour tortilla with a filling and wrapped like an envelope

Calf fries-Mountain oysters, prairie eggs

Catfish -Texans favorite fish

Chicken-fried-Cooking method used almost exclusively in Texas

Chili-Meat dish with no beans

Chimichanga-Tortilla with a filling, wrapped like an envelope and deep-fried

Church key-Bottle opener

Cookin' on the front burner-Doing something well; doing it now

Cork it-Be quiet

Cowboy Kool-Aid-Beer

Cream gravy-In Texas considered a main course or beverage; made with pan drippings, flour, salt and pepper; can be eaten on any food

Dinner -Noon meal

Dude-Unflattering term for someone who thinks he's smarter than a Texan

Eggs-Hen apples

Enchilada-Tortilla with filling, rolled into log shape with chile sauces and cheese poured on top

Everthang-Everything

Fixin'-Cookin' as in "I'm fixin dinner."

Fixin' to-Will do something soon; "I'm fixin' to fix dinner."

Flauta-Tortilla with filling, rolled very tightly and deep-fried

Frijoles-(Free ho lees) Pinto beans

Fry your own bacon-Mind your own business.

Full as a tick-Dined sufficiently

Gringo-Derogatory name for non-Mexicans

Hasta luego-Good-bye

Hell-A unit of measure; expletive; "That pepper's hotter 'n hell." "I'm madder 'n hell." "Hell yes, I'm gonna eat it."

Hominy-Corn used to make grits, corn flakes, corn syrup, cornstarch and corn oil

Humility-A character trait unknown or unpracticed by most Texas cooks and most Texans

Hunard-100; "My chicken laid a hunard eggs yesterd'y."

Jalapenos-(Hal a pain yos) Head honcho of peppers; sometimes referred to as Mexican bullets

Jerky-Dead meat

Kemosabe-Friend; amigo

Larrupin' good-Real good

Littl' lady-Female; littl' darlin'

Marinades-Seasonings and ingredients used to tenderize tough cuts of meat

Masa harina-Dried and ground corn flour

Masa-Fresh corn dough

Meskun-Mexican; "Meskun food sure is good."

Mesquite-(Ma skeet) Wood used to smoke meat; ol' scrub tree to stay away from

Mind your biscuits-Mind your own business.

Muy beaucoup-Thank you very much

Muy bueno-Very good

Norther-Cold weather; Good time to have a "Bowl of Red"

Pecans-(Pu cons) There are no "pee cans" in Texas.

Quesadilla-Tortilla filled with cheese, meat and/or salsa, folded in half and heated until cheese melts

Rubs-Seasonings used to flavor meats, not tenderize them

Salsa Cruda-Fresh tomato salsa with tomatoes, onion, jalapenos, serranos, cilantro and garlic

Salsa Verde-Fresh tomatillos, cilantro and jalapenos finely diced and served in bowl with chips

Salsa-Mixture of vegetables, fruits or nuts used to fill tortillas and to accompany Mexican dishes

Slather-Put it all over; use a lot of it; "It's sa good, you can just slather it all over that chicken."

Sop-Noun meaning mixture of seasonings and ingredients used to flavor meat; verb meaning what you do with your bread when there's some gravy leftover

Sopaipillas-Favorite sweet; triangles of flour, sugar and baking powder deep-fried and served hot with honey and powdered sugar

Stick to your ribs-What pinto beans will do before they talk behind your back

Supper-Night meal

Sure as shootin'.-A sure thing; definitely; "She's fixin' chili tonight, sure as shootin'!"

Taco-Soft or crispy tortilla filled with meat, cheese, tomatoes, onions and salsa

Tex-Mex-See page 6.

That gravy needs a little tightenin' up.-The gravy is too thin; gravy needs to be thickened

The whole enchilada-Everything; all

Tortilla -Flat bread made from corn or flour and used in Mexican cooking

Tortilleria-A tortilla factory

Tostada -Tortilla that is flat or basket-shaped and fried crisp

Whistleberries-Pinto beans

Yes siree bob-Yes; definitely

You betcha-Yes; "Can you come to supper tonight? You betcha!"

You betcha-You're welcome. "Thank you for bringin' in the groceries." "You betcha."

OFFICIAL STATE SYMBOLS

State Bird .... **Mockingbird**

State Flower........................... **Bluebonnet**

State Tree.............................. **Pecan**

State Dish............................. **Chili**

State Fruit .... **Texas red grapefruit (Ruby Red)**

State Mammals ....**Armadillo (small); Longhorn (large)**

State Native Pepper: ....**Chiltepin**

State Pepper: .... **Jalapeno**

State Vegetable: ....**Texas sweet onion (1015)**

State Plant:............................ **Prickly pear cactus**

State Shrub:........................... **Crape myrtle**

State Sport:........................... **Rodeo**

Boy Howdy!

◆—✦—◆

Salsas

Teasers ★ Brews

Official Pepper of the State of Texas

JALAPENO

Official Native Pepper of the State of Texas

CHILTEPIN

≈⊷✦⊶≈ *Slim's Tidbit:* ≈⊷✦⊶≈

"There's no safer place than behind momma's apron."

PEPPERS

⮜⮜⟶⮞⮞ Slim's Tidbit: ⮜⮜⟶⮞⮞

"If the chiltepin pepper is called the "mother of all peppers", then it's tha hottest mother in tha world. Naturally, a pepper with such distinction is gonna come from Texas.

Obviously, then tha head honcho of all peppers in tha world is tha hal a pain yo. There's just no use for tha word pepper when you're talking bout hal a pain yos. We just say hal a pain yo cause if you don't know it's a pepper you're already in trouble and nobody I knows gonna keep you from tha privlege of findin' out it's a pepper."

Jalapenos are about 2 to 3 inches long with a tapered end and about a 1-inch shoulder (the part under the stem). They are deep green, sometimes with tan or brown stripes. Jalapenos have a mild to hot flavor and are easy for most people to enjoy. In 1990 a Texas A&M professor developed a mild jalapeno. Today, Texas is the largest producer of jalapenos in the US.

The chiltepin pepper is native to Texas and is thought to be the oldest known pepper in the capsicum genus. It is the hottest wild pepper in the Americas and considered by most highly intelligent people to be hotter than the habanero.

Poblano peppers are about 3 to 5 inches long and rounded instead of elongated. They are dark green and ripen to reddish-brown. They are very mild

Serranos are small peppers about 1 to 1½ inches long and not very wide. They are very hot.

Habaneros are considered by some to be the hottest pepper in the world, but that is incorrect. The hottest pepper in the world is the Official Native Pepper of The State of Texas called the chiltepin.

The chipotle pepper is a smoke-dried jalapeno and is excellent for sauces, salsas, pastas and soups. It has a full-flavored heat that is very satisfying.

Ancho peppers are dried poblanos and are about 3½ to 5 inches long and about 3 inches wide. They are mild to slightly hot and a dark, reddish-brown color.

New Mexico Reds (or Colorados, means red in Spanish) are also called chile colorado. They are the peppers you see in the traditional ristras used for decorations in kitchens and homes in Texas border towns, New Mexico and Arizona. The chile is essential for some of the red chile sauces and has a wonderful earthy flavor with a crisp, mild heat.

SALSA

In *Classic Tex-Mex and Texas Cooking*, basic salsas mean tomatoes, onions, and jalapenos or chopped green chilies or both, usually uncooked, but not always. Sauces, on the other hand, are usually cooked and have a blended, smooth texture and are served over foods.

Here are some of the basic salsas found on Texas tables. As Tex-Mex expands its horizons, so do salsas expand their flavors and uses. Think beyond the cup of salsa and chips on the table at a Mexican restaurant. Think fresh and think salsas served with beef, chicken, pork, beans and many vegetables. You will discover new flavors and gain a new appreciation for the salsa we so often take for granted.

★FRESH TOMATO SALSA

4 medium tomatoes, diced
2 to 4 green onions with tops, diced
1 to 2 jalapeno peppers
½ cup snipped cilantro leaves
Juice of 1 small lime
1 teaspoon sugar

✪ Dice tomatoes and onions in large mixing bowl to save juices.

✪ Wash jalapenos, remove stems and seeds and dry with paper towels. Dice jalapenos and add to tomatoes.

✪ Combine with all other ingredients and 1 teaspoon salt and refrigerate for about 15 to 20 minutes.

✪ Remove from refrigerator and taste. If tomatoes are too tart, add a little sugar to cut the tartness. Refrigerate about 30 minutes more to blend flavors and serve. Yield: 1½ cups.

★SALSA VERDE

Tomatillos are great, little green tomatoes with paper-thin husks on the outside.

6 to 8 tomatillos
2 large red bell peppers, stemmed, seeded, diced
2 to 3 jalapenos
¾ cup snipped fresh cilantro leaves
Juice of 1 small lime

✪ Remove husks from tomatillos, wash and dry with paper towels. In large mixing bowl dice tomatillos and bell peppers.

✪ Wash jalapenos, remove seeds and dry with paper towels. Dice jalapenos and add to tomatillos.

✪ Combine all other ingredients and 1 teaspoon salt and refrigerate for about 30 minutes. Yield: About 1½ cups.

SALSA DE CHILE VERDE

4 to 6 tomatoes, diced
4 green onions with tops, diced
2 to 3 jalapenos, stemmed, seeded, diced
1 (7 ounce) can diced green chilies
½ cup snipped fresh cilantro leaves
1 teaspoon freshly ground black pepper

✪ Combine all ingredients and 1 teaspoon salt. Adjust seasonings for your own tastes. Yield: About 2 cups.

SALSA PICANTE

1 bunch green onions with tops, diced
2 cloves garlic, minced
1 to 2 jalapeno peppers, stemmed, seeded, diced
1 tablespoon corn oil
1 (7 ounce) can diced green chilies
1 teaspoon vinegar
1 (4 ounce) tomato sauce

✪ In skillet cook onions, garlic and jalapenos in oil until onions are translucent.

✪ Remove from heat and add green chilies, vinegar, tomato sauce, a little salt and pepper and serve. Yield: 1½ cups.

★SALSA CILANTRO

4 tomatoes, diced
4 green onions with tops, diced
1 green bell pepper, stemmed, seeded, diced
1 red bell pepper, stemmed, seeded, diced
1 to 2 jalapeno peppers, stemmed, seeded, diced
¾ to 1 cup snipped fresh cilantro leaves
1 to 2 tablespoons fresh lime juice

✪ Mix all ingredients and a little salt and pepper and refrigerate before serving. Yield: 2 cups.

BLACK BEAN SALSA

1 (15 ounce) can black beans, drained
4 to 6 green onions with tops, diced
½ to ¾ cup snipped fresh cilantro leaves
1 to 2 cloves garlic, minced
1 tablespoon oil
1 teaspoon fresh lime juice

✪ Mix all ingredients and refrigerate before serving. Yield: 2 cups.

MANGO-JALAPENO SALSA

2 ripe mangoes, peeled, diced
4 green onions with tops, diced
2 jalapeno peppers, stemmed, seeded, diced
¼ cup snipped fresh cilantro leaves
¼ to ½ cup fresh lime juice
1 teaspoon cumin

✪ Combine all ingredients and a little salt and refrigerate before serving.
Yield: 1½ cups.

TIP: Make sure mangoes are ripe. Taste mango to see if it is tart next to the
seed. If so, only use flesh away from seed.

★QUICK-DRAW SALSA

When you are pressed for time, this is a very quick salsa to make.

4 tomatoes, chopped
4 green onions with topped, chopped
1 (7 ounce) can chopped green chilies

✪ Combine all ingredients and a little salt and pepper and serve.
Yield: 2 cups.

MEXICALI-CORN SALSA

1 (11 ounce) can Mexicorn, drained
½ cup sour cream
¾ cup mayonnaise
1 (4 ounce) can chopped green chilies
⅓ cup finely chopped green onions with tops
⅓ cup finely chopped sweet red bell pepper
¼ cup chunky salsa
1 tablespoon ground cumin
½ teaspoon seasoned salt
1 (12 ounce) package shredded cheddar cheese
Several dashes hot sauce, optional

✪ In large bowl, combine all ingredients and stir well to blend.

✪ Refrigerate several hours before serving. Serve with crackers.
  Yield: 3 cups.

 *Editor's Choice*

★TEXAS PICO DE GALLO

*The Texas 1015 SuperSweet Onion is the star in this terrific salsa. It's great over
quesadillas, fajitas, tacos, black-eyed peas or grilled entrees.*

2 cups diced tomatoes
1 cup diced Texas 1015 SuperSweet Onions
  or Texas SpringSweet Onions
2 cups diced ripe avocado
⅓ cup snipped fresh cilantro

✪ Mix all ingredients and ½ teaspoon each of salt and pepper in bowl
  and refrigerate several hours before serving.

✪ Serve as an appetizer with chips or onion pieces or as a side dish.
  Yield: 4½ cups.

TOSTADOS

1 package (12 count) corn tortillas
Oil

✪ Cut corn tortillas like a pizza in pie-shaped triangles.

✪ In heavy skillet or griddle with hot oil, drop tortilla triangles, turn once and fry until crispy.

✪ Remove from oil, drain on paper towel and sprinkle a little salt on top. Serve immediately with salsas and dips. Yield: 48 chips.

TEXAS JALAPENO SPREAD

2 jalapeno peppers, seeded, finely chopped
3 green bell peppers, seeded, finely chopped
1½ cups white vinegar, divided
6½ cups sugar
½ teaspoon cayenne pepper
1 (6 ounce) package liquid fruit pectin
Cream cheese and crackers

✪ In blender, combine jalapeno pepper, green peppers and ¾ cup vinegar and process until pureed.

✪ Pour into large saucepan and add sugar, ¾ cup vinegar and cayenne pepper. Bring mixture to boil and stir constantly.

✪ Stir in fruit pectin and boil 1 minute longer, stirring constantly.

✪ Remove from heat, skim off foam and pour into sterilized jars. To serve, spread cream cheese on crackers and top with jalapeno spread. Yield: 3 half-pint jars.

JALAPENO EGGS

8 hard-boiled eggs
Sliced pickled jalapenos with liquid
1 small onion, separated into rings
1 (2 ounce) jar chopped pimentos
¾ cup white vinegar
¾ cup jalapeno juice

✪ While eggs are still hot, peel eggs and place in wide-mouth, 1-quart jar and alternate with jalapenos, onion and pimentos. Put lid on jar.

✪ Bring vinegar and jalapeno juice to boil. (Always use equal parts vinegar and jalapeno juice – no substitutes.) Immediately pour over eggs-onion in jar.

✪ Work fast. If eggs cool, they will toughen. Cover and refrigerate about 2 weeks. Yield: 8 eggs.

CAYENNE COOKIES

1 cup (2 sticks) butter, softened
1 (16 ounce) package shredded sharp cheddar cheese
2 cups flour
2 cups crispy rice cereal
¼ teaspoon garlic powder
¼ teaspoon cayenne pepper

✪ Preheat oven to 350°.

✪ Mix butter and cheese. Add all other ingredients and ¼ teaspoon salt and mix well.

✪ Drop by teaspoonfuls on unsprayed cookie sheet. Bake for 12 to 15 minutes. Yield: 3 dozen cookies.

ENCHILADA DIP

½ onion, chopped
1 pound lean ground beef
1 tablespoon oil
1 teaspoon minced garlic
1 (10 ounce) can enchilada sauce
1 (1 ounce) envelope dry enchilada sauce
1 (6 ounce) can tomato sauce
1 (16 ounce) package shredded Velveeta® cheese

✪ In large skillet, saute onion and brown ground meat in oil.

✪ Add garlic, canned enchilada sauce, dry enchilada sauce, tomato sauce and ½ cup water.

✪ Simmer about 5 to 10 minutes or until water cooks out.

✪ Add Velveeta cheese to beef mixture, stirring constantly, until cheese melts.

✪ Serve in chafing dish with chips. Yield: 1½ pints dip.

" **S**paniards planted their brightly colored flag in Texas soil as early as the 16th century, bringing with them European cultural building blocks for a new frontier. For three centuries they dominated. Along with the Spanish troops came horses, cattle and other domesticated animals unknown to the Indians. They brought guns and gunpowder for making war as well as new concepts of law and government for keeping the peace... Spaniards mapped the territory and christened it Tejas, a Caddo-Indian word for friend."

The Melting Pot: Ethnic Cuisine in Texas
The Institute of Texan Cultures of The University of Texas at San Antonio

CHILI-BEEF DIP

1 onion, finely chopped
1 pound lean ground beef
1 tablespoon oil
1 tablespoon chili powder
1 (10 ounce) can chili-beef soup
1 (10 ounce) can fiesta nacho cheese soup

✪ In skillet, saute onion and beef in oil and season with chili powder and ½ teaspoon salt.

✪ Add soups and simmer on very low heat for about 25 minutes, stirring occasionally. Serve hot with chips. Yield: 1½ pints dip.

EASY CHILI DIP

1½ pounds lean ground beef
1 onion, chopped
2 tablespoons chili powder
2 tablespoons cumin
1 teaspoon garlic powder
1 (10 ounce) can chili-beef soup without beans
1 (16 ounce) jar mild Mexican Cheese Whiz®

✪ In large skillet saute beef and onion and drain.

✪ Add chili powder, ½ teaspoon salt, cumin, garlic powder, chili-beef soup and 1 soup can of water.

✪ Simmer about 20 minutes or until water cooks out. Add Cheese Whiz and stir until cheese melts. Serve hot in chafing dish with chips. Yield: 2 pints.

TEJAS-SAUSAGE DIP

1 pound hot, ground sausage
1 pound ground beef
1 onion, chopped
1 (10 ounce) can tomatoes and chilies
2 pounds Velveeta® cheese, cubed
1 (10 ounce) can cream of mushroom soup

✪ Brown sausage, ground beef and onion in skillet and drain.

✪ Add tomatoes and chilies and Velveeta cheese to meat mixture. Cook on low heat and stir constantly until cheese melts.

✪ Add cream of mushroom soup and mix well. Serve hot. Yield: 1 quart dip.

TEXAS BLACK-EYED PEA DIP

4 (15 ounce) cans black-eyed peas, drained
1 onion, chopped
2 teaspoons minced garlic
1 (10 ounce) can tomatoes and green chilies
1 (8 ounce) package shredded Mexican Velveeta® cheese
1 cup (2 sticks) butter

✪ Combine peas, onion, garlic, tomatoes and green chilies in blender and mix well.

✪ In large double boiler or heavy saucepan, combine Velveeta cheese and butter.

✪ On low heat, cook until cheese melts. Stir in black-eyed pea-mixture. Pour into chafing dish. Serve with corn chips. Yield: 2 quarts.

WILD WEST DIP

1 pound hot sausage
1 (10 ounce) can tomatoes and green chilies
1 (1 pound) box Velveeta® cheese, chopped

✪ Brown sausage and drain. Add tomatoes, green chilies and Velveeta cheese to sausage mixture.

✪ Cook over low heat until cheese melts and stir constantly.

✪ Serve in chafing dish along with chips. Yield: 1 pint dip.

★CHILE CON QUESO

3 onions, minced
¼ cup (½ stick) butter
2 (4 ounce) cans diced, green chilies, drained
1½ cups milk
1 (1 pound) box Velveeta® cheese, cubed
1 (8 ounce) package shredded cheddar cheese
1 (8 ounce) package shredded Mexican 4-cheese blend
1 to 2 teaspoons hot sauce

✪ Saute onion in butter until onion is translucent. Add green chilies and slowly pour in milk and 1 cup water. Cook until mixture begins to boil.

✪ Reduce heat to low and add cheeses, stirring constantly, until cheeses melt. Add hot sauce and mix well.

✪ Pour into large bowl, cover and refrigerate overnight.

✪ Reheat in double boiler and serve hot with chips. Yield: 2 pints.

Editor's Choice

★ORIGINAL HOT CHEESE DIP

1 onion, finely chopped
¼ cup (½ stick) butter
1 (10 ounce) can chopped tomatoes and green chilies
1 (4 ounce) can chopped green chilies
1 (2 pound) box Velveeta® cheese
Chips

✪ In large saucepan, combine onion and butter. Cook slowly until onion is clear.

✪ Add tomatoes and green chilies and green chilies and stir well.

✪ Cut Velveeta cheese in chunks and add to onion-tomato mixture. Heat mixture on low until cheese melts, stirring constantly.

✪ Serve hot or at room temperature with chips. Yield: 1½ pints.

"The first Spanish population was comprised of families of Spanish soldiers and settlers from the Canary Islands and northern Mexico. They established the towns of San Antonio, La Bahia (later Goliad) and Nacogdoches."

The Melting Pot: Ethnic Cuisine in Texas
The Institute of Texan Cultures of The University of Texas at San Antonio

SOMBRERO DIP

¼ cup (½ stick) butter
6 fresh mushrooms, chopped
½ onion, chopped
3 ribs celery, very finely chopped
½ sweet red bell pepper, very finely chopped
1 (10 ounce) can cream of mushroom soup
2 (6 ounce) rolls garlic cheese, cubed
1 (10 ounce) package frozen chopped broccoli, cooked, drained

✪ In skillet with butter, saute mushrooms, onion, celery and bell pepper.

✪ Stir in mushroom soup and cheese and mix well until cheese melts.

✪ Fold in cooked, well drained broccoli. Stir on low heat until ingredients mix well and are hot. Serve from chafing dish with chips. Yield: 1½ pints.

BEAN-CHEESE TACO DIP

1 (10 ounce) can bean and bacon soup
1 (8 ounce) carton sour cream
½ (8 ounce) package cubed Velveeta® cheese
1 (1 ounce) envelope taco seasoning mix
1 teaspoon minced garlic

✪ In large saucepan, combine soup, sour cream, Velveeta cheese cubes, taco mix and garlic.

✪ On low heat, cook, stirring constantly, until cheese melts. Serve warm with chips. Yield: 1 pint.

FIESTA SHRIMP DIP

1 (8 ounce) package cream cheese, softened
½ cup mayonnaise
1 (6 ounce) can shrimp, chopped
1 rib celery, finely chopped
2 green onions, finely chopped
¼ teaspoon garlic powder
1 teaspoon lemon juice
¼ teaspoon Creole seasoning

✪ Blend cream cheese and mayonnaise.

✪ Stir in shrimp, celery, onion, garlic powder, lemon juice, ¼ teaspoon salt and Creole seasoning. Mix well and refrigerate.

✪ Serve with chips or vegetable sticks. Yield: 1 cup.

EASY CHEESY BEAN DIP

1 (15 ounce) can refried beans
1 teaspoon minced garlic
1 cup milk
1 (16 ounce) package Mexican Velveeta® cheese

✪ In large saucepan, combine beans, garlic and milk and stir on low heat until smooth.

✪ Cut cheese in chunks and add to bean mixture. On low heat, stir until cheese melts. Serve warm with chips. Yield: 2 pints.

TIP: Use this dip for soft, bean tacos or burritos. Spread bean dip on flour tortillas, add chopped tomatoes, chopped jalapenos and shredded cheese, roll up and pig out.

WEST TEXAS DIP

2 (8 ounce) packages cream cheese, softened
¼ cup lime juice
1 tablespoon ground cumin
½ to 1 teaspoons cayenne pepper
1 (8 ounce) can whole kernel corn, drained
1 cup chopped walnuts
1 (4 ounce) can chopped green chilies
3 green onions with tops, chopped

✪ In mixing bowl, whip cream cheese until fluffy and beat in lime juice, cumin, 1 teaspoon salt and cayenne pepper.

✪ Stir in corn, walnuts, green chilies and onions and mix well.

✪ Refrigerate several hours or overnight. Serve with tortilla chips. Yield: 1 pint.

VAQUERO BEAN DIP

1 (15 ounce) can refried beans
2 to 3 pickled jalapenos, stemmed, seeded, minced
1 tablespoon chili powder
1 teaspoon cumin
1 teaspoon white cider vinegar
1 small onion, minced

✪ Blend refried beans, jalapenos, chili powder, cumin and vinegar until mixture is a smooth consistency.

✪ Add onion and stir well. Serve with chips, in burritos or on nachos. Yield: 1 pint.

TIP: Make your own refried beans. Recipe is on page 105.

LAYERED TACO DIP

½ cup mayonnaise
1 cup sour cream
1 (1½ ounces) package taco seasoning
2 (14 ounce) cans refried beans with green chilies
2 (8 ounce) packages frozen guacamole
2 tomatoes, chopped
2 green onions with tops, chopped
1 (8 ounce) package shredded cheddar cheese
1 (4 ounce) can chopped ripe olives, drained
Chips

✪ Mix mayonnaise, sour cream and taco seasoning and set aside.

✪ On large platter or 9 x 13-inch glass dish, spread refried beans as first layer of dip.

✪ Spread guacamole as second layer and cover with sour cream-mayonnaise mixture.

✪ Sprinkle layer of chopped tomatoes, layer of green onions, layer of cheese and layer of olives. Serve with chips. Yield: 1 quart.

"At the beginning of the 19th century Spain began to lose her New World possessions. Texas and the rest of Mexico fought and won freedom from European control during the second decade of the century. For the next 15 years Texas was a part of the Republic of Mexico."

The Melting Pot: Ethnic Cuisine in Texas
The Institute of Texan Cultures of The University of Texas at San Antonio

GALVESTON BAY CRAB SPREAD

1 (10 ounce) can cream of shrimp soup
1 (8 ounce) package cream cheese, cubed
¼ cup finely minced green onions
1 cup mayonnaise
2 (.25 ounce) envelopes unflavored gelatin
2 (6 ounce) cans crabmeat, washed, picked
1 cup very finely chopped celery
¼ cup finely chopped ripe olives, optional

✪ In saucepan, combine soup, cream cheese and green onions. Heat on low and stir constantly until cheese melts. Fold in mayonnaise and mix.

✪ Dissolve gelatin in 1 cup cold water. When it dissolves, blend into soup mixture and heat until mixture is warm. Stir in crabmeat, celery and olives.

✪ Pour into 8-inch mold or loaf pan. Refrigerate several hours or overnight.

✪ When ready to serve, remove from mold, slice and spread on wheat crackers. Serves 8.

TAMALES QUICK DIP

1 (15 ounce) can tamales
1 (16 ounce) can chili without beans
1 cup salsa
2 (5 ounce) jars Cheez Whiz®
1 cup finely chopped onion

✪ Mash tamales with fork. Put all ingredients in saucepan, heat and combine. Serve hot with crackers or chips. Yield: 1 quart

ROAST BEEF SANDWICH SPREAD

2 to 2½ cups leftover roast
½ cup drained sweet pickle relish
3 celery ribs, chopped
2 hard-boiled eggs, chopped
1 teaspoon seasoned salt
1 teaspoon seasoned pepper
1 to 1½ cups mayonnaise

✪ Place roast pieces in blender and pulse several times to chop roast.

✪ Add pickle relish, celery, eggs, salt and pepper and mix well. Stir in enough mayonnaise to blend roast-egg mixture.

✪ Spread on bread to make sandwiches or on crackers for snack. Yield: 1 quart

HOT-TO-TROT JALAPENO PIE

1 (8 ounce) can jalapeno peppers, seeded, chopped
1 (8 ounce) package shredded cheddar cheese
4 eggs, beaten

✪ Preheat oven to 400°.

✪ Place peppers in sprayed 9-inch pie plate. Sprinkle cheese over peppers. Add ½ teaspoon salt and ¼ teaspoon pepper to eggs and pour over cheese.

✪ Bake for 20 minutes. Let pie sit at room temperature for about 10 minutes. Cut into thin pie wedges to serve. Searves 8.

 *Editor's Choice*

STOMPIN' GOOD JALAPENO SQUARES

2 (4 ounce) cans jalapeno peppers, seeded, chopped
1 pound bacon, fried, crumbled
1 (12 ounce) package shredded Mexican 4-cheese blend
1 (4 ounce) can sliced mushroom stems and pieces, drained
10 eggs, well beaten

✪ Preheat oven to 325°.

✪ Line bottom of sprayed 9 x 13-inch baking dish with jalapenos.

✪ Sprinkle bacon pieces, cheese and mushrooms in layers. Pour beaten eggs over top.

✪ Cook for about 25 to 30 minutes or until center is firm.

✪ Let stand 15 minutes before slicing. Cut into squares and serve hot. Serves 8.

TIP: If you want a mild "hot", just use 1 can jalapenos.

"For over 300 years, from the 1500's to the 1800's, Texas shared a common history with Mexico. During most of this time Texas was a sparsely settled, frontier province along the northern border. The few Europeans who lived in the territory were concentrated along the San Antonio River and in east Texas. These people were primarily ranchers, small businessmen and professionals."

The Melting Pot: Ethnic Cuisine in Texas
The Institute of Texan Cultures of The University of Texas at San Antonio

GIT ALONG LITTLE DOGIES

1 cup ketchup
1 cup plum jelly
1 tablespoon lemon juice
2 tablespoons prepared mustard
2 (5 ounce) packages tiny smoked sausage

✪ In saucepan, combine all ingredients except sausages. Heat and mix well.

✪ Add sausages and simmer for 10 minutes. To serve, use cocktail toothpicks. Yield: 1½ pints.

RANCH ROLL-UPS

2 (8 ounce) packages cream cheese, softened
⅓ cup mayonnaise
1 (1 ounce) envelope ranch salad dressing mix
¼ cup finely chopped green onions with tops
¼ cup very finely grated pecans
1 (2 ounce) jar pimentos, well drained
10 to 12 (8 inch) flour tortillas
20 to 22 very thin slices deli ham

✪ In mixing bowl, beat cream cheese, mayonnaise and ranch dressing mix until smooth. Add onions, pecans and pimentos and stir well.

✪ Spread about 3 tablespoons over each tortilla and top each with 2 ham slices. Roll up tightly and wrap in plastic wrap.

✪ Refrigerate several hours or overnight. Unwrap and cut into ¾-inch slices. Serves 10 to 12.

★EASY GRINGO GUACAMOLE

More guacamole is eaten in Texas than any other state in the U.S.

3 ripe avocados, peeled, seeded
1 tablespoon lemon juice
1 teaspoon minced garlic
1 small tomato, chopped
½ cup grated onion
¼ cup hot salsa

✪ Place all ingredients, 1 teaspoon salt and a little pepper in blender or food processor and pulse 2 to 3 times.

✪ Process until guacamole is chunky, but not pureed. Serve with chips. Yield: 1 cup.

★SPICY GUACAMOLE

4 ripe avocados, peeled, seeded
½ cup mayonnaise
1 firm, ripe tomato, seeded, very finely chopped
¼ cup finely minced onion
1½ tablespoons lemon juice
¼ teaspoon ground cumin
¼ teaspoon cayenne pepper
¼ teaspoon chili powder

✪ Mash avocados, combine with mayonnaise and mix well with hand mixer.

✪ Add tomato, onion, lemon juice, seasonings and 1 teaspoon salt and blend thoroughly. Store, covered, in refrigerator. Yield: 1 cup.

CHEESE-BISCUIT BANDITS

1 (6 ounce) jar Old English cheese
1 cup (2 sticks) butter
½ teaspoon cayenne pepper
¼ teaspoon baking powder
2⅓ cups flour
1 cup very finely chopped pecans

✪ With mixer, blend cheese and butter. Add 1 teaspooon salt, cayenne pepper, baking powder and flour and mix well. (Biscuit dough will be very stiff.) Stir in pecans.

✪ Make 4 logs about 8 inches long. Wrap in wax paper and refrigerate in refrigerator until ready to bake.

✪ Cut slices ⅛-inch thick and place on lightly sprayed baking sheet. Bake at 325° for about 20 minutes. Yield: 2 dozen.

"In 1824 the Mexican government approved a constitution patterned after that of the United States, which, among other things, permitted Anglo-Americans immigration to Texas. Ten years later it was repudiated by President Antonio Lopez de Santa Anna who assumed dictatorial powers. All over Mexico there were small revolutions against the Santa Anna government, most of which were quickly crushed by the army...

In early 1836 Texans decided that complete separation from Mexico was the best course, and in April, Texas won her independence at San Jacinto.

The Melting Pot: Ethnic Cuisine in Texas
The Institute of Texan Cultures of The University of Texas at San Antonio

★EASY CHALUPAS

12 flat, crispy corn tortillas
1 (15 ounce) can refried beans
1 (12 ounce) package shredded cheddar cheese
1 cup chopped lettuce
2 tomatoes, chopped
1 large onion, chopped
Salsa

✪ Preheat oven to 300°.

✪ Separate tortillas, spread refried beans over each tortilla and sprinkle cheese on top.

✪ Place on baking sheets and heat just until cheese melts.

✪ Remove from oven and top with lettuce, tomato, onion and salsa. Serve immediately. Serves 8.

TIP: **If you cannot find the crispy, flat tortillas, buy the soft ones and fry in hot oil until they are crispy. Drain thoroughly, top with refried beans and cheese and heat. Add lettuce, tomato, onion and salsa and serve immediately.**

SWEET TEXAS ONIONS

2 to 3 Texas 1015 SuperSweet onions or 5 sweet onions, sliced
1 cup sugar
½ cup white vinegar
⅔ cup mayonnaise
1 teaspoon celery salt

✪ Soak onions in sugar, vinegar and 2 cups water for about 3 hours and drain.

✪ Toss with mayonnaise and celery salt and serve on crackers. Serves 6 to 8.

 *Editor's Choice*

TEXAS PARTY MIX

1 (12 ounce) box Corn Chex®
1 (12 ounce) box Wheat Chex®
1 (12 ounce) box Rice Chex®
2 to 3 cups thin pretzel sticks
2 (12 ounce) cans mixed nuts
2 (12 ounce) cans peanuts
1 to 1¼ cups (2 to 2½ sticks) butter
2 tablespoons seasoned salt
1 tablespoon garlic powder
2 tablespoons hot sauce
2 tablespoons Worcestershire sauce
1 to 2 teaspoons cayenne pepper

✪ Preheat oven to 225°.

✪ Mix Corn Chex, Wheat Chex, Rice Chex, pretzels, mixed nuts and peanuts in large roasting pan.

✪ Melt butter and stir in seasoned salt, garlic powder, hot sauce, Worcestershire and cayenne pepper. Pour over cereal mixture and mix well.

✪ Bake for about 2 hours, stirring every 30 minutes. Cool and store in airtight containers. Serves 10 to 20.

The best preserved collection of Victorian iron-front buildings with structural and decorative ironwork in the U.S. can be found on the Strand north of Broadway in Galveston.

TEXAS-SPICED PECANS

⅓ cup (5 tablespoons) butter
2 teaspoons ground cumin
¼ teaspoon cayenne pepper
2 tablespoons sugar
3½ cups pecan halves

✪ Preheat oven to 300°.

✪ In large skillet, melt butter and add cumin, cayenne, sugar and
1 teaspoon salt. Cook, stirring constantly, for 1 minute.

✪ Remove from heat, stir in pecans and mix until sauce coats all pecans.

✪ Spread on large cookie sheet or baking pan. Bake for 25 to 30
minutes or until light brown, stirring occasionally.

✪ Cool and store in airtight container. Serves 6 to 10.

San Antonio was first established as a mission in 1719, but gained prominence in
1836 when 180 volunteers, including Jim Bowie and Davy Crockett under the
command of William Travis, defended "The Alamo" while greatly outnumbered
by Santa Anna's troops in an effort to win Texas' independence from Mexico.

The largest pecan tree in the world and the national champion pecan tree is just
north of Weatherford and has a span of more than 150 feet.

★JALAPENO JELLY

1 green bell pepper, finely ground
¼ cup fresh jalapeno peppers, ground
1 cup cider vinegar
5 cups sugar
1 (6 ounce) box liquid fruit pectin
Green food coloring

✪ In large saucepan, combine bell pepper, jalapeno peppers, vinegar and sugar. Boil for about 4 minutes.

✪ Cool 1 minute and stir in fruit pectin and a few drops of green coloring. Pour into 5 (6 ounce) sterilized, hot jelly jars and seal.

✪ Serve over cream cheese with crackers. Yield: 5 half-pint jars.

ALMOND-TEA PUNCH

½ cup lemon juice
1¼ cups sugar
2 tablespoons almond extract
1 tablespoon vanilla
1¼ cups strong tea
1 quart ginger ale, refrigerateed
1 lemon, thinly sliced

✪ In saucepan, combine lemon juice, sugar, almond extract, vanilla and tea.

✪ Bring to boil, remove from heat and pour into large pitcher.

✪ Add 2 cups cold water and ginger ale. Serve over crushed ice with lemon slices for garnish. Yield: 1½ quarts.

SPARKLING CRANBERRY PUNCH

2 quarts cranberry juice cocktail
1 (6 ounce) can frozen lemonade, thawed
1 quart ginger ale, refrigerateed
Red food coloring, optional
Ice ring for punch bowl

✪ In large pitcher, combine cranberry juice cocktail and lemonade
and refrigerate.

✪ When ready to serve, pour cranberry mixture into punch bowl, add
ginger ale and stir well. Serves 8 to 12.

TIP: You can freeze an ice ring of water and red food coloring or ice ring of
cranberry juice.

SUMMERTIME PUNCH

1 (3 ounce) package lime gelatin
1 (6 ounce) can frozen limeade, thawed
1 (6 ounce) can frozen lemonade, thawed
1 quart orange juice
1 quart pineapple juice
1 tablespoon almond extract
2 to 3 drops green food coloring
1 liter ginger ale, refrigerateed

✪ Dissolve lime gelatin in 1 cup boiling water and stir well.

✪ In large pitcher or 1-gallon bottle, combine dissolved gelatin, limeade,
lemonade, orange juice, pineapple juice, almond extract and food
coloring and refrigerate.

✪ When ready to serve, place juice mixture in punch bowl and add
ginger ale. Yield: 4 quarts.

WINTER-SPICED CIDER

1 gallon apple cider
2 cups orange juice
¼ cup maple syrup
½ teaspoon lemon extract
5 cinnamon sticks
3 teaspoons whole cloves
½ teaspoon whole allspice

✪ In large roasting pan or kettle, combine apple cider, orange juice, maple syrup and lemon extract.

✪ Place cinnamon sticks, cloves and allspice in piece of cheesecloth. Bring up corners, tie with string to form bag and add to roasting pan.

✪ Cook, uncovered, over medium heat (do not boil) for 15 to 20 minutes. Discard spice bag. Serves 16 to 22.

TEXAS COOK-OFFS

Houston Livestock Show and Rodeo World Championship BBQ Cook-Off		January
LaSalle County Fair and Wild Hog Cook-Off	Cotulla	March
World's Largest Rattlesnake Round-Up and Brisket and Chili Cook-Offs	Sweetwater	March
National Championship Chuck Wagon Cook-Off	Abilene	March
CASI Texas Ladies State Chili Championship	Seguin	April
Cowtown CASI Pod Chili Cook-Off and Chisholm Trail BBQ Cook-Off	Fort Worth	June
International BBQ Cook-Off	Taylor	August
Fresh Chili Pepper Festival	Austin	September
Shrimporee	Aransas Pass	September
National Championship Chuck Wagon Cook-Off	Lubbock	September

 *Editor's Choice*

CAPPUCCINO PUNCH

¼ cup instant coffee granules
¾ cup sugar
3 pints milk
1 pint half-and-half cream
1 quart chocolate ice cream, softened
1 quart vanilla ice cream, softened

✪ In bowl, combine coffee granules and sugar and stir in 1 cup boiling water. Cover and refrigerate.

✪ When ready to serve, pour refrigerateed coffee mixture into 1-gallon punch bowl.

✪ Stir in milk and half-and-half cream. Add scoops of both ice creams and stir until most of ice cream melts. Serves 16 to 22.

TEXAS COOK-OFFS

World Championship Barbecue Goat Cook-Off..............Brady.......September
National Cowboy Symposium Barbecue Cook-Off........Lubbock.......September
Republic of Texas Chilympiad ....San Marcos.......September
State Fair of Texas BBQ and Chili Cook-Off....................Dallas..........October
Czhilispiel..Flatonia..........October
Pendery's Chili Cook-Off...Fort Worth..........October
Brinkman Backyard BBQ Cook-Off.....................Grand Prairie..........October
Henly Memorial Ladies State
     Chili Championship of Texas .... Lukenback..........October
World Championship Shrimp Cook-Off....................Port Isabel..........October
World Championship Wild Hog Barbecue Cook-Off......Crowell.......November
Original Terlingua International Frank X Tolbert-
     Wick Fowler Memorial Chili Cook-Off .... Terlingua.......November

RUBY RED-STRAWBERRY-MANGO SMOOTHIE

2 Texas Ruby Red grapefruit
1 cup chopped, ripe mango
1 medium banana
1 (8 ounce) carton strawberry-banana yogurt
2 tablespoons honey
½ teaspoon white vanilla extract
Ice

✪ Slice grapefruit into halves and squeeze enough fresh juice to equal 1⅓ cups.

✪ Pour juice into blender and add mango, banana, strawberry yogurt, honey, white vanilla extract and about ½ cup ice.

✪ Turn blender to blend and process several times. Add another ½ cup ice and process until smooth. Serves 8.

★HOT DR. PEPPER

Cold or hot, it's a Texas favorite.

1 Dr. Pepper
1 slice lemon

✪ Pour Dr. Pepper in cup and zap it in microwave or heat it in saucepan on stove.

✪ Serve piping hot with slice of lemon.

Dr. Pepper was invented in 1885 in Waco, Texas at the Old Corner Drug Store and was first bottled in Dallas. The oldest Dr. Pepper bottling company in the world is located in Dublin, Texas and was built in 1891.

Editor's Choice

HOMEMADE AMARETTO

3 cups sugar
1 pint vodka
3 tablespoons almond extract
1 tablespoon vanilla

✪ Combine sugar and 2¼ cups water in large saucepan. Bring mixture to boil and reduce heat.

✪ Simmer 5 minutes, stirring occasionally, and remove from stove.

✪ Add vodka, almond and vanilla. Stir to mix well.

✪ Store in airtight jars. Yield: 1½ pints.

Editor's Choice

HOMEMADE KAHLUA

1 cup instant coffee granules
4 cups sugar
1 quart vodka
3 tablespoons Mexican vanilla

✪ In large saucepan, combine 3 cups hot water and coffee and mix well. Add sugar and boil for 2 minutes. Turn off heat and cool.

✪ Add vodka and vanilla. Pour into bottle or jar and store in refrigerator. Shake occasionally. Yield: 2 quarts.

SANGRIA

1 (750 mL) bottle red table wine
1 (10 ounce) bottle sparkling water
Juice of 1 lemon
Juice of 1 orange
¼ to ½ cup sugar
Strawberries
Orange slices
Lemon slices
Lime slices

✪ In large pitcher, pour red wine, sparkling water, 1 cup water and juices of 1 lemon and 1 orange. Add sugar to taste.

✪ Put most of fruit slices in pitcher and reserve some for individual glasses.

✪ Pour into wine glasses and garnish with fruit slices. Serves 8.

ALAMO SPLASH

2 ounces tequila
2 ounces orange juice
2 ounces pineapple juice
Splash lemon-lime soda

✪ Mix with cracked ice and pour into one Collins glass.

Slim's Tidbit:

"Just lookin' at this recipe 'minds me a tha ol' boy who got so drunk he had to hold on to tha grass 'fore he could lean against tha ground."

 *Editor's Choice*

BLOODY MARIA

2 ounces tequila
4 ounces tomato juice
2 dashes lemon juice
2 dashes hot sauce
2 dashes celery salt

✪ Pour over cracked ice and stir vigorously.

✪ Pour into one old-fashioned glass with ice cubes. Serve with lemon slice.

⟞⟐⟝

CACTUS BERRY

1 ounce tequila
1 ounce red wine
1 ounce triple sec liqueur
6 ounces sour mix
1 splash lemon-lime soda
1 dash lime juice

✪ Pour over cracked ice and pour into one salt-rimmed, margarita glass.

⟞⟐⟝

★CHAPALA

This is a favorite with Mexican-Texans.

2½ ounces tequila
2 teaspoons grenadine
Dash triple sec liqueur
2 tablespoons orange juice
2 tablespoons lime juice

✪ Mix in shaker with ice, tequila, grenadine, triple sec, orange juice and lime juice and pour over ice in highball glass. Serves 2.

SO WHO'S MARGARITA?

According to legend, the margarita was concocted by a bartender in Ciudad Juarez, just across the Texas border from El Paso. He confused a woman's cocktail order and mistakenly mixed tequila, triple sec liqueur and lime juice with crushed ice. She raved about the new concoction and need we say more… her name was Margarita.

EASY FROZEN STRAWBERRY MARGARITA

1 (10 ounce) can frozen strawberries
1 (6 ounce) can frozen limeade
1 (6 ounce) can tequila
Ice

✪ Pour strawberries, limeade, tequila and ice into blender and process until smooth.

✪ Add enough ice to fill blender. Pour into margarita glasses. Serves 6.

TEQUILA SUNRISE

2 ounces tequila
4 ounces orange juice
1 ounce grenadine

✪ Pour tequila and orange juice over ice into highball glass.

✪ Slowly pour in grenadine and allow to settle. Stir to finish the sunrise. Serves 2.

Slim's Tidbit:
"Now this is a drink worth bendin' an elbow for."

Hot Dang!

RISE & SHINE

HOT BREADS

Official Fruit of The State of Texas

RUBY RED GRAPEFRUIT

Slim's Tidbit:

*"Texas eggs are so big it dudn't take
many of 'em to make a dozen."*

★BREAKFAST TACOS

6 to 8 flour tortillas
1 cup frozen hash browns, thawed
1 onion, minced
1 bell pepper, minced
1 (4 ounce) can chopped green chilies, drained, optional
4 eggs
2 to 3 tablespoons milk
Salsa

✪ Wrap flour tortillas in foil and warm in oven at 200°.

✪ On griddle or large skillet, cook hash browns. Brown onions, bell pepper and green chilies.

✪ Beat eggs with milk.

✪ Move potato mixture to one side, pour in beaten eggs and scramble.

✪ Mix hash browns, onions, bell peppers, chilies and eggs and spoon into flour tortilla. Roll tortilla and serve hot with salsa. Serves 6.

El Paso is located between two mountain ranges on the banks of the Rio Grande River. Early Spanish explorers named the north-south route through the mountains, Camino Real, and believed it to be a good trade route. It was used as a trade highway for more than 300 years.

The real Old West of Texas lies in the westernmost part of the state from El Paso to Midland-Odessa to San Angelo and the Big Bend National Park in the south. There are small towns, real cowboys, real honky-tonks, Longhorn cattle and lots of frontier.

★BREAKFAST BURRITOS

6 large flour tortillas
½ pound ground sausage
2 fresh green onions, chopped
5 large eggs, slightly beaten
2 tablespoons milk
⅔ cup shredded cheddar cheese
Salsa

✪ Preheat oven to 250°.

✪ Wrap tortillas tightly in foil and heat in oven for about 15 minutes.

✪ In skillet, brown sausage and onions, drain and set aside.

✪ Combine eggs, milk, and a little salt and pepper. Pour into skillet and cook, stirring constantly.

✪ When eggs are still slightly moist, remove from heat. Add sausage-onion to eggs.

✪ Spoon sausage-egg mixture into middle of tortillas. Top with cheese and about 1 tablespoon salsa, roll up and tuck ends inside the rolls. Serves 6.

EASY BREAKFAST EGGS

6 eggs
2 cups milk
1 pound sausage, cooked, browned
¾ cup grated Velveeta®
6 slices white bread, trimmed, cubed

✪ Preheat oven to 350°.

✪ Beat eggs, add milk, sausage and cheese and pour over bread. Mix well, pour into sprayed 9 x 13-inch baking pan and cover with foil.

✪ Bake at 350° for 20 minutes. Remove foil, turn oven to 375° and bake for another 10 minutes. Serves 6.

★HUEVOS RANCHEROS

½ cup chopped onion
½ teaspoon minced garlic
3 tablespoons bacon drippings
4 tomatoes, seeded, finely chopped, drained
Minced jalapenos peppers to taste
6 eggs
6 fried tortillas

✪ Saute onion and garlic in bacon drippings. Add tomatoes, peppers and ½ teaspoon salt.

✪ Cover and simmer for 10 minutes.

✪ Fry each egg and place one on each tortilla. Spoon sauce over each egg and serve. Serves 6.

The Texas Folklife Festival is the state's largest celebration of the state's ethnic diversity. More than 30 ethnic groups showcase their culture's food, crafts and traditions. The festival is held in San Antonio in August.

Mission San Francisco de la Espada's Aqueduct in San Antonio is the only functioning aqueduct remaining from the Spanish Colonial Period in the U.S. It was completed in 1745.

★RANCHERO SAUCE

Ranchero sauce is a general all-purpose sauce for enchiladas, barbecue, eggs and anything else you want to put it on. I guess you could call it "your basic Tex-Mex ketchup".

4 tomatoes, peeled, seeded, chopped
4 cloves garlic, crushed
1 onion, minced
1 New Mexico Red dried, chili pepper, ground, divided
2 teaspoon snipped fresh oregano

✪ Pour tomatoes, garlic juice and onion in skillet, cook over medium-low heat until onions are clear and tomatoes are mushy, about 15 to 20 minutes, and stir frequently.

✪ Mash tomatoes, add half of ground chili pepper, oregano and ½ cup water and stir well. Remove from heat and let sauce rest for about 30 minutes, stirring occasionally. Taste and add ground chili pepper and salt, if needed. Serve warm. Yield: 1½ cups.

BRUNCH BISCUITS

½ cup (1 stick) butter, melted
2 cups self-rising flour
1 (8 ounce) carton sour cream

✪ Preheat oven to 350°.

✪ Combine all ingredients and mix well. Spoon in sprayed, miniature muffin tins.

✪ Bake for 15 minutes or until light brown. Yield: 8 biscuits.

TIP: These biscuits are so rich they do not need butter.

BREAKFAST BREAK

1 pound hot sausage, cooked, crumbled
2 tablespoons dried onion flakes
1 (8 ounce) package shredded cheddar cheese
1 cup biscuit mix
4 eggs, well beaten
2 cups milk

✪ Preheat oven to 350°. Place cooked crumbled sausage in sprayed
9 x 13-inch glass baking dish. Sprinkle with onion and cheese.

✪ In mixing bowl, combine biscuit mix, ¼ teaspoon each of salt and
pepper, and eggs and beat well. Add milk and stir until it blends well.
Pour over sausage mixture and bake covered for 35 minutes. Serve
with toast or biscuits and jelly. Add 1 (8 ounce) can whole kernel
corn, drained and serve for brunch. Serves 8.

QUESADILLA PIE

1 (4 ounce) can chopped green chilies, drained
½ pound ground sausage, cooked
1 (12 ounce) package shredded cheddar cheese
3 eggs, well beaten
1½ cups milk
¾ cup biscuit mix
Hot salsa

✪ Preheat oven to 350°.

✪ Sprinkle green chilies, cooked sausage and cheddar cheese in sprayed
9-inch pie pan.

✪ In separate bowl, mix eggs, milk and biscuit mix and pour over green
chilies, sausage and cheese.

✪ Bake for 30 minutes. To serve top each slice with salsa. Serves 6.

BANDIT-SAUSAGE RING

This is a pretty impressive presentation and feast.

1 pound mild sausage
1 pound hot sausage
1½ cups crushed cracker crumbs
2 eggs, slightly beaten
½ cup milk
½ cup finely minced onion
1 cup finely chopped apple
12 scrambled eggs

✪ Preheat oven to 350°.

✪ Thoroughly combine sausage, cracker crumbs, eggs, milk, onion and apple. Press tightly into sprayed ring mold and turn out onto a shallow baking pan with sides.

✪ Bake for 50 minutes. Drain well before placing on serving platter.

✪ Fill center with scrambled eggs and serve immediately. Serves 8 to 10.

TIP: This recipe may be made in advance, baked partially for 30 minutes, drained and refrigerateed until ready to serve. Continue baking for 20 to 30 minutes until it is hot.

RANCH SAUSAGE AND GRITS

1 cup quick-cooking grits
1 pound pork sausage, cooked, drained
1 onion, chopped, cooked
1 cup salsa
1 (8 ounce) package shredded cheddar cheese, divided

✪ Preheat oven to 350°.

✪ Cook grits according to package directions. Combine grits, sausage, onion, salsa and half cheese. Spoon into sprayed 2-quart baking dish.

✪ Bake for 15 minutes. Remove from oven and add remaining cheese on top of casserole. Bake another 10 minutes and serve hot. Serves 8.

★GREEN CHILE GRITS

The best way to eat grits is with green chilies. A jalapeno on the side is not too bad either.

1½ cups quick-cooking grits
¾ cup (1½ sticks) butter
1 (16 ounce) package shredded cheddar cheese
1 teaspoon seasoned salt
½ teaspoon white pepper
1 (4 ounce) can chopped green chilies
1 (2 ounce) jar chopped pimentos, drained
3 eggs beaten

✪ Preheat oven to 350°.

✪ In large saucepan, cook grits in 6 cups boiling water, stirring occasionally, until grits thicken.

✪ Stir in butter, cheese, seasonings, 1 teaspoon salt, green chilies and pimentos. Continue to stir and cook on low heat until butter and cheese melt.

✪ Remove from heat and fold in beaten eggs. Pour into sprayed 9 x 13-inch baking dish. Bake for 1 hour. Serves 8.

CRABMEAT QUICHE

3 eggs, beaten
1 (8 ounce) carton sour cream
1 (6 ounce) can crabmeat, rinsed
½ cup shredded Swiss cheese
1 (9-inch) piecrust

✪ Preheat oven to350°.

✪ In bowl, combine eggs and sour cream. Blend in crabmeat and cheese and add a little garlic salt and pepper.

✪ Pour into piecrust and bake for 35 minutes. Serves 6

GRAHAM-STREUSEL COFFEE CAKE

2 cups graham cracker crumbs
¾ cup chopped pecans
¾ cup firmly packed brown sugar
1½ teaspoons ground cinnamon
¾ cup (1½ sticks) butter
1 (18 ounce) box yellow cake mix
1 cup water
½ cup oil
3 eggs

GLAZE:
1½ cups powdered sugar

✪ Preheat oven to 350°.

✪ Mix graham cracker crumbs, pecans, brown sugar, cinnamon and butter and set aside.

✪ Blend cake mix, 1 cup water, oil and eggs on medium speed for 3 minutes.

✪ Pour half batter in sprayed, floured 9 x 13-inch pan. Sprinkle with half reserved crumb mixture. Spread remaining batter evenly over crumb mixture. Sprinkle remaining crumb mixture over top.

✪ Bake for 45 to 50 minutes.

GLAZE:

✪ Mix powdered sugar and 2 tablespoons water and drizzle over cake while still hot. Serves 8 to 10.

★CATTLE TRAIL SOURDOUGH STARTER

1 package dry yeast
2 cups flour
2 cups warm water

✪ Combine ingredients in large plastic, glass or ceramic bowl (not metal) and mix well.

✪ Cover loosely with cheesecloth or old dishtowel and put in warm place for 48 hours. Stir several times each day to mix ingredients.

✪ Starter will increase in volume a little, but not the way bread rises. Store starter in refrigerator.

✪ When ready to make bread or biscuits, stir well and remove amount needed. Replenish starter with 1 cup flour and 1 cup water, mix well and store in refrigerator.

OPTIONAL: Another way to replenish sourdough starter calls for 1 cup flour, 1 cup milk and ¼ cup sugar. Since cowboys did not put milk in their biscuits, we stuck with the real chuckwagon-cowboy version.

The Stockyards National Historic District still looks like the Old West and is home to the Cowtown Coliseum, the first indoor rodeo arena in the world, and Billy Bob's Texas, the largest honky-tonk in the world.

The only daily cattle drive in the world is held about noon every day down Exchange Avenue in the Stockyards National Historic District in Fort Worth. A dozen or two, 2,000-pound Texas Longhorns are driven down the red-brick street by cowboys dressed in 19th century duds to their grazing area near the West Fork of the Trinity River.

★SOURDOUGH BULLETS

Biscuits were very important on cattle drives and the mood of the wranglers often depended on good biscuits from the chuck wagon cook.

1 cup flour
2 teaspoons sugar
1 teaspoon baking powder
¼ cup (3 tablespoons) bacon grease or butter
1 cup Cattle-Drive Sourdough Starter (page 58)

✪ Preheat oven to 400°.

✪ In large bowl, combine flour, sugar, baking powder and ½ teaspoon salt and mix well. Pour in a little bacon grease at a time and stir to mix well.

✪ Form well in center of dough and pour in sourdough starter. Stir well to mix.

✪ Lay out wax paper on counter and sprinkle flour over paper. Flour your hands and knead dough on wax paper just until smooth.

✪ Press dough out to make large piece about ½ inch thick. Use small, thin-brimmed glass and cut out biscuits.

✪ Pour a little bacon grease in 9 x 13-inch baking pan and coat bottom of pan. Place each biscuit in pan, then turn them over so both sides have a little bacon grease on them.

✪ Cover with cup towel or wax paper and place in warm area for about 30 minutes.

✪ Bake for about 25 minutes or until biscuits are light brown. Serve hot with lots of butter and honey. Serves 8.

⤙⤙⤙ Slim's Tidbit: ⤙⤙⤙

"The way a chuck wagon cook earned his reputation was by his biscuits. If tha biscuits weren't any good, nobody was happy and it was a looooong, cattle drive. If tha biscuits were good, everybody was happy and tha drive wan't a half-bad adventure."

 *Editor's Choice*

BISCUITS AND SAUSAGE GRAVY

This is about as down-home as you can get and it is every bit as good as you can imagine.

3 cups biscuit mix
4 cups milk, divided
½ pound pork sausage
2 tablespoons (¼ stick) butter
⅓ cup flour

✪ Preheat oven to 400°.

✪ Combine biscuit mix and ¾ cup milk and stir. Roll dough on floured wax paper to ¾-inch thickness and cut with biscuit cutter. Place on sprayed baking sheet.

✪ Bake for 12 to 15 minutes or until golden.

✪ For gravy, brown sausage and drain, reserving pan drippings in skillet. Set sausage aside.

✪ Add butter to drippings and melt. Add flour and cook 1 minute, stirring constantly.

✪ Gradually add remaining milk, cook over medium heat, stirring constantly until mixture thickens. Stir in ½ teaspoon each of salt and pepper and add sausage.

✪ Cook until heated, stirring constantly. Serve sausage gravy over cooked biscuits. Serves 8.

Pecos Cantaloupes grow in the southernmost tip of Texas and are known for their sweet flavor. The best way to choose a cantaloupe is to smell the stem end. The cantaloupe will taste the way it smells.

TEXAS GARLIC TOAST

1 loaf thick Texas bread
1 tablespoon garlic powder
¼ cup finely chopped parsley or 1 tablespoon dried parsley flakes
1 teaspoon marjoram leaves
½ cup (1 stick) butter, melted
1 cup parmesan cheese

✪ Preheat oven to 225°.

✪ Slice bread in 1-inch slices diagonally.

✪ In small bowl combine garlic powder, parsley, marjoram leaves and butter and mix well. Use brush to spread mixture on bread slices and sprinkle with parmesan cheese.

✪ Place on baking sheet and bake for about 1 hour. Yield: 14 to 16 slices.

CRUNCHY BREAD STICKS

1 (8 count) package hot dog buns
1 cup (2 sticks) butter, melted
Garlic powder
Paprika

✪ Preheat oven to 225°.

✪ Slice each bun in half lengthwise.

✪ Use pastry brush to butter all bread sticks and sprinkle a little garlic powder and a couple sprinkles of paprika on each.

✪ Place on baking sheet and bake for 45 minutes. Serves 8.

TEXAS HUSH PUPPIES

2 cups yellow cornmeal
1 cup flour
2 teaspoons baking powder
2 tablespoons sugar
1 cup corn, drained
1 small onion, very finely minced
2 eggs
1 cup milk
2 tablespoons bacon drippings
Oil for frying

✪ In bowl, combine cornmeal, flour, 2 teaspoons salt, baking powder and sugar and mix well. Add corn, onion, eggs, milk and bacon drippings and mix until they blend well.

✪ Heat oil in deep fryer and drop batter about the size of golf balls in oil. Cook until golden brown and drain on paper towels. Serves 8.

Editor's Choice

JUST PLAIN OL' CORNBREAD

1 cup flour
1 cup yellow cornmeal
¼ cup sugar
4 teaspoons baking powder
2 eggs
1 cup milk
¼ cup oil

✪ Preheat oven to 375°.

✪ Mix all ingredients and ¾ teaspoon salt and blend well. Pour into sprayed 9 x 13-inch baking dish. Bake for 30 minutes or until light brown. Serves 10 to 12.

★MEXICAN CORNBREAD
Boy Howdy!

1 cup flour
1 cup cornmeal
4 teaspoons baking powder
1 egg
1 cup milk
1 (15 ounce) can cream-style corn
¼ cup oil
1 jalapeno, chopped
1 (8 ounce) package shredded 4-cheese blend, divided

✪ Preheat oven to 350°.

✪ In bowl, combine all ingredients, except cheese; add 1 teaspoon salt and stir well.

✪ Pour half batter into sprayed 9 x 13-inch baking pan and sprinkle half cheese over batter. Top with remaining batter and remaining cheese.

✪ Bake for 50 to 60 minutes or until light brown. Serves 10 to 12.

CHEDDAR CORNBREAD

2 (8½ ounce) packages cornbread-muffin mix
2 eggs, beaten
1 cup plain yogurt
1 (14 ounce) can cream-style corn
½ cup shredded cheddar cheese

✪ Preheat oven to 400°.

✪ In bowl, combine cornbread mix, eggs and yogurt and blend well. Stir in corn and cheese.

✪ Pour into sprayed 9 x 13-inch baking dish. Bake for 18 to 20 minutes or until slightly brown. Serves 10 to 12.

★TEX-MEX CORNBREAD

I mean to shout!

2 eggs, beaten
1 cup sour cream
1 (15 ounce) can cream-style corn
½ cup oil
1 (8 ounce) package shredded cheddar cheese
1 (4 ounce) can chopped green chilies
3 tablespoons chopped onion
3 tablespoons chopped bell pepper
1½ cups cornmeal
2½ teaspoons baking powder

✪ Preheat oven to 350°.

✪ Mix eggs, sour cream, creamed corn, oil, cheese, chilies, onion and bell pepper.

✪ Mix dry cornmeal, baking powder and 1 teaspoon salt and quickly add to sour cream mixture. Pour in sprayed 9 x 13-inch baking pan and bake for 45 minutes. Serves 10 to 12.

Editor's Choice

HOT WATER CORNBREAD

1½ cups cornmeal
1 egg, beaten
¼ cup (½ stick) butter, melted
Oil

✪ Pour 1¼ cups boiling water over cornmeal and 1 teaspoon salt, stir very well and cool. Stir in egg and butter.

✪ Drop by tablespoonfuls into skillet with a little oil and form into small patty shapes with spoon.

✪ Brown on both sides and drain on paper towels. Serve hot with butter. Serves 6.

A DIFFERENT HOT WATER CORNBREAD

2 cups cornmeal
½ teaspoon baking soda
3 tablespoons butter
2 eggs, separated

✪ Preheat oven to 350°.

✪ Pour 1½ cups boiling water over cornmeal, 1 teaspoon salt, baking soda and butter and stir vigorously to remove lumps. (Mixture will be thick.)

✪ Cool slightly and stir in beaten egg yolks. Fold in stiffly beaten egg whites and drop by tablespoonfuls onto sprayed baking sheet.

✪ Bake for about 7 to 8 minutes or until light brown. Serves 8.

TEXAS BEER BREAD

3 cups self-rising flour
¼ cup sugar
1 (12 ounce) can beer, room temperature
1 egg, beaten
2 tablespoon butter, melted

✪ Preheat oven to 350°.

✪ In bowl, combine flour, sugar and beer; just mix until well blended. Spoon into 9 x 3-inch loaf pan. To give bread a nice glaze, combine egg and 1 tablespoon water; brush top of loaf with mixture. Bake for 40 to 45 minutes; when removing loaf from oven, brush top with melted butter. Serves 8.

SPICY CORNBREAD TWISTS

3 tablespoons (⅓ stick) butter
½ cup cornmeal
¼ teaspoon cayenne pepper
1 (11 ounce) can refrigerated soft breadsticks

✪ Preheat oven to 350°.

✪ Place butter in pie plate and melt butter in oven. Remove from oven as soon as butter melts.

✪ On wax paper, mix cornmeal and cayenne pepper.

✪ Roll breadsticks in butter and in cornmeal mixture. Twist breadsticks according to label directions and place on large cookie sheet.

✪ Bake for 15 to 18 minutes. Serves 6.

BROCCOLI CORNBREAD

1 (10 ounce) package frozen chopped broccoli, thawed
2 (6 ounce) boxes cornbread muffin mix
¾ cup (1½ sticks) butter, melted
1 medium onion, chopped
4 eggs, slightly beaten
1 cup carton cottage cheese

✪ Preheat oven to 350°.

✪ Mix all ingredients. Bake in sprayed 9 x 13-inch baking pan for 25 to 30 minutes.

✪ Batter will rise as it cooks and fall when it is done. This freezes well. Serves 10-12.

GLAZED-LEMON BREAD

½ cup shortening
1 cup sugar
2 eggs
1½ cups flour
1 teaspoon baking powder
½ cup milk
1 teaspoon lemon extract
Peel of 2 lemons, grated
½ cup chopped pecans

GLAZE:
Juice of 2 lemons
¼ cup sugar

✪ Preheat oven to 325°.

✪ In large bowl cream shortening and sugar. Add eggs and beat thoroughly.

✪ Sift flour, baking powder and pinch of salt and add, alternately with milk, to creamed mixture.

✪ Add lemon extract and grated lemon peel and fold in chopped pecans.

✪ Pour in sprayed, floured, 9 x 5-inch loaf pan and bake for 60 to 65 minutes. Test with toothpick for doneness.

FOR GLAZE:

✪ Combine lemon juice and sugar in saucepan and bring to boil.

✪ Pour over bread while it is still hot in pan. Use toothpick to pierce bread so glaze will soak into loaf. Serves 6 to 8.

BANANA-PINEAPPLE LOAF

This is wonderful sliced, buttered and toasted for breakfast.

1 cup (2 sticks) butter, softened
1 cup sugar
4 eggs
1 cup ripe, mashed bananas
4 cups sifted flour
2 teaspoons baking powder
1 teaspoon baking soda
1 (15 ounce) can crushed pineapple with liquid
1 (7 ounce) can flaked coconut, optional
1 cup chopped pecans

✪ Preheat oven to 350°.

✪ Cream butter and sugar, add eggs and mix well. Stir in bananas.

✪ Sift flour, baking powder, baking soda and ½ teaspoon salt and add to butter mixture. Fold in pineapple, coconut and pecans.

✪ Pour in 2 sprayed, floured, 9 x 5-inch loaf pans. Bake for 1 hour and 10 minutes. Test with toothpick for doneness. Serves 12 to 16.

TIP: For lunch, spread cream cheese on slices of banana-pineapple bread, cut into thirds and serve as finger sandwiches.

Who says Texas is flat?
The highest point in Texas is Guadalupe Peak at 8,749 feet above sea level. Its twin peak is El Capitan at 8,085 feet above sea level. They are in Guadalupe Mountains National Park in the western-most part of Texas.

DELICIOUS PUMPKIN BREAD

1 cup oil
3 cups sugar
4 eggs
1 teaspoon vanilla
1 (15 ounce) can pumpkin
2 teaspoons baking powder
2 teaspoons ground cinnamon
¼ teaspoon ground allspice
3 cups flour
1 cup chopped dates
1½ to 2 cups chopped pecans

✪ Preheat oven to 350°.

✪ In mixing bowl, combine oil and sugar, add eggs one at a time, beating well after each addition.

✪ Add vanilla and pumpkin and mix well.

✪ Sift together 1 teaspoon salt, baking powder, cinnamon, allspice and flour. Add to sugar-pumpkin mixture and beat well with electric mixer. Stir in dates and pecans.

✪ Pour into 2 sprayed, floured 9 x 5-inch loaf pans.

✪ Bake for 70 to 75 minutes and test for doneness with toothpick. Serves 12 to 16.

TIP: This is fabulous served with lots of butter or for sandwiches with cream cheese filling.

Texas is larger than any country in Europe and is the 5th largest producer of oil among all the oil-producing countries in the world.

ZUCCHINI-PINEAPPLE BREAD

3 eggs, beaten
2 cups sugar
1 cup oil
2 teaspoons vanilla
2 cups grated zucchini
3 cups flour
1 teaspoon baking soda
3 teaspoons ground cinnamon
½ teaspoon baking powder
1 cup chopped pecans
1 (8 ounce) can crushed pineapple, drained
1 (8 ounce) carton spreadable cream cheese

✪ Preheat oven to 325°.

✪ Mix eggs, sugar, oil and vanilla and mix well.

✪ Add remaining ingredients except cream cheese, add 1 teaspoon salt and mix well and pour in 2 sprayed, floured, 9 x 5-inch loaf pans.

✪ Bake for 60 minutes or until toothpick inserted in center comes out clean. Cool several minutes.

✪ To serve, slice and spread with cream cheese. Serves 12 to 16.

Editor's Choice

VERY BERRY STRAWBERRY BREAD

3 cups sifted flour
2 cups sugar
1 teaspoon baking soda
1 tablespoon ground cinnamon
3 large eggs, beaten
1 cup oil
1¼ cups pecans, chopped
2 (10 ounce) packages frozen sweetened strawberries with juice,
thawed
1 (8 ounce) package light cream cheese, softened

✪ Preheat oven to 350°.

✪ In large mixing bowl, combine flour, sugar, 1 teaspooon salt, baking soda and cinnamon. Add remaining ingredients except cream cheese.

✪ Pour in 2 sprayed, floured 5 x 9-inch loaf pans.

✪ Bake for 1 hour or toothpick inserted comes out clean. Cool several minutes before removing from pan.

✪ To serve, slice bread and spread cream cheese between 2 slices. For finger sandwiches, cut in smaller pieces. Serves 12 to 16.

The Strawberry Capital of Texas is Poteet. The Poteet Strawberry Fetival is the largest agricultural festival in Texas.

MAPLE-SPICE MUFFINS

1¼ cups flour
1½ cups whole wheat flour
½ cup quick-cooking oats
1 teaspoon baking soda
2 teaspoons baking powder
2 teaspoons ground cinnamon
½ teaspoon ground cloves
2 eggs
1 (8 ounce) carton sour cream
1 cup maple syrup
1 cup packed brown sugar
½ cup oil
½ teaspoon maple flavoring, optional
1 banana, mashed
1 cup chopped walnuts

✪ Preheat oven to 375°.

✪ In mixing bowl, combine both flours, oats, baking soda, baking powder, cinnamon and cloves and mix well.

✪ Add eggs, sour cream, maple syrup, brown sugar, oil, maple flavoring and mashed banana and stir well by hand.

✪ Add walnuts and pour into 24 paper-lined muffin tins. Bake for 18 to 20 minutes. Yield: 24 muffiins.

FRESH BLUEBERRY MUFFINS

1¼ cups sugar
2 cups flour
1½ teaspoons baking powder
½ cup (1 stick) butter, softened
1 egg, beaten
1 cup milk
1½ cups fresh blueberries
½ cup chopped pecans

✪ Preheat oven to 375°.

✪ In large bowl, combine sugar, flour, baking powder and ½ teaspoon salt. Cut in softened butter until mixture is coarse.

✪ Stir in egg and milk and beat well. Gently fold in blueberries and pecans, but do not beat.

✪ Spoon into sprayed muffin pan and bake for 35 minutes or until light brown. Yield: 12 muffins.

GINGERBREAD MUFFINS

1 (18 ounce) box gingerbread mix
1 egg
2 (1½ ounce) boxes seedless raisins

✪ Preheat oven to 350°.

✪ Combine gingerbread mix, 1¼ cups lukewarm water and egg and mix well. Stir in raisins and pour into sprayed muffin tins half full.

✪ Bake for 20 minutes or until toothpick comes out clean. Yield: 12 to 14 muffins.

LARRUPPIN' GOOD SECRET MUFFINS

FILLING:
1 (8 ounce) package cream cheese, softened
1 egg
½ cup sugar
1 tablespoon grated orange peel

MUFFINS:
1 cup (2 sticks) butter, softened
1¾ cups sugar
3 eggs
3 cups flour
2 teaspoons baking powder
1 cup milk
1 teaspoon almond extract
1 cup slivered almonds

✪ Preheat oven to 375°.

✪ Beat cream cheese, egg, sugar and orange peel and set aside.

✪ Cream butter and sugar until light and fluffy. Add eggs one at a time, beating after each addition.

✪ Stir flour and baking powder together. Add flour and milk alternately to butter-sugar mixture, beginning and ending with flour.

✪ Add almond extract and fold in almonds.

✪ Fill 26 lightly sprayed muffin tins half full of muffin batter. Spoon about 1 teaspoon cream cheese in each muffin. Top filling with muffin batter.

✪ Bake for 20 to 25 minutes or until muffins are light brown. Yield: 26 muffins.

★Scratch Corn Tortillas

3 cups masa harina
1¾ to 2 cups hot water

✪ Mix masa harina with water, a little at a time, until you can form dough into large, soft ball.

✪ Cover bowl with cup towel and take out enough dough to make smaller balls about 2 inches in diameter. Keep bowl covered to keep moisture in dough. Add water if necessary.

✪ Put small ball in between 2 pieces of plastic wrap and roll out flat to about 6 to 7 inches in diameter and about ¼ inch thick. Seal plastic wrap so dough will not dry out.

✪ Heat heavy skillet or griddle with a little oil and remove plastic from tortilla before putting in hot oil.

✪ Cook in hot oil for about 30 seconds, then turn to other side and cook for another 30 seconds or until tortillas appear to be crispy. (They will get crispier after removed from skillet.) Remove from skillet and drain on paper towels.

✪ Taste and add a little salt if desired. Yield: 18 to 20 tortillas.

★SCRATCH FLOUR TORTILLAS

These are great with butter when they are hot straight off the griddle.

4 cups flour
1 teaspoon baking powder
3 to 4 tablespoons bacon drippings, corn oil or olive oil

✪ In large bowl combine flour, 1 to 2 teaspoons salt and baking powder.

✪ Pour in a little bacon drippings and ½ cup warm water and mix well. Add enough drippings and more warm water to make dough pliable enough to form into large, solid ball.

✪ Cover ball in bowl with cup towel and let dough rest about 5 to 10 minutes in a warm place.

✪ Divide dough into smaller, round balls about 3 to 4 inches in diameter.

✪ Heat heavy skillet or griddle with a little oil.

✪ Flour your hands and mash each ball between your hands into flat tortillas about 7 or 8 inches in diameter and about ¼ inch thick. Shape into round circles and place in hot oil.

✪ Cook on each side until brown spots appear. Do not cook them long enough to get crispy. If tortillas puff up a little, press them down with spoon or spatula. Drain on paper towels, but do not stack until they cool.

✪ Serve immediately while they are hot or cool to reheat at a later time. Yield: 18 to 22 tortillas.

Sure as Shootin!

❖

Rabbit Food
Sips & Slurps
Whistleberries
Sidekicks

Official Dish of The State of Texas

CHILI

⤐⤐⤐ *Slim's Tidbit:* ⤐⤐⤐

"Anytime you can pass my house, I'd sure appreciate it."

SAVORY SPINACH SALAD

½ cup oil
½ cup red wine vinegar
3 tablespoons ketchup
¼ cup sugar
½ teaspoon garlic powder
½ teaspoon dry mustard
1 (10 ounce) package fresh spinach
4 hard-boiled eggs, sliced
8 slices bacon, crisply cooked, crumbled
1 cup sliced fresh mushrooms
1 small red onion, sliced
1 (8 ounce) can sliced water chestnuts, drained
Croutons

✪ Combine oil, vinegar, ketchup, sugar, 1 teaspoon salt, garlic, dry mustard and a little pepper to make dressing. Refrigerate at least 6 hours before serving.

✪ Wash, drain and tear spinach in bite-size pieces.

✪ When ready to serve, toss spinach with eggs, bacon, mushrooms, onion, water chestnuts and dressing. Top with croutons and serve. Serves 6.

Texans of German descent are in the fourth largest ethnic group in Texas. German immigrants started coming to Texas in the 1830's and continued until the Civil War. German culture and traditions endure today because of the large number of Germans who made Texas their home.

GRANDMA'S HOT GERMAN POTATO SALAD

½ pound bacon
3 pounds new potatoes
1 tablespoon flour
⅔ cup plus 1 tablespoon cider vinegar
3 to 4 tablespoons sugar
¾ cup chopped celery
¾ cup chopped onion
3 hard-boiled eggs
Paprika

✪ Cook bacon, crumble and set aside. Save bacon drippings.

✪ Gently cook potatoes in boiling water until just tender. Drain and set aside.

✪ Return ½ cup bacon drippings to skillet over low heat, add flour and stir until flour dissolves.

✪ Add vinegar and ⅓ cup water, stir constantly and simmer for about 1 minute or until it thickens. Turn heat off and add sugar and stir until it dissolves.

✪ When potatoes are just cool enough to handle, slice one-third into large casserole dish and add one-third each of celery, onion and bacon.

✪ Sprinkle lightly with salt and pepper and drizzle several spoonsful of dressing over top. Repeat this process 2 more times, but reserve 3 spoonfuls of dressing.

✪ Slice eggs over top and drizzle remaining dressing over eggs. Sprinkle lightly with paprika for garnish. Serve warm. Serves 8 to 10.

Mrs. Terry Arndt (Barbara)

The Best of Lone Star Legacy Cookbooks, Austin Junior Forum, Published by Cookbook Resources, LLC

POTATO-SALAD REUNION

7 medium potatoes
⅓ cup Italian dressing
¾ cup sliced green onions with tops
3 hard-boiled eggs, chopped
1 cup chopped celery
1 (4 ounce) jar diced pimento, drained
½ cup pickle relish, drained
1 cup mayonnaise
½ cup sour cream
1 tablespoon prepared mustard
1 teaspoon seasoned salt
1 teaspoon seasoned pepper
½ teaspoon chili powder
Paprika

✪ Boil potatoes with peels on until tender. While still warm, peel, slice and cover with dressing. Refrigerate several hours.

✪ Add onions, eggs, celery, pimento and pickle relish and toss.

✪ Add mayonnaise, sour cream, mustard, ½ teaspoon salt and seasonings, except paprika; fold in potato mixture and refrigerate.

✪ Place in crystal bowl and garnish with paprika. Serves 8.

With 254 Texas has more counties than any other state in the U.S. There are 41 counties in Texas that are bigger than the state of Rhode Island.

A DIFFERENT TACO SALAD

1 pound ground beef
1 large onion, chopped
1 (16 ounce) can red kidney beans, rinsed, drained
1½ teaspoons cumin
½ to ¾ head lettuce
2 tomatoes, chopped
1 avocado, diced
3 green onions with tops, chopped
1 (3 ounce) can sliced ripe olives, drained
1 (2 ounce) jar chopped pimentos, drained
1 (16 ounce) package shredded Monterey Jack cheese
1 (10 ounce) bag corn chips
Catalina salad dressing

✪ In skillet, saute beef and onions and drain grease. Add beans, cumin,
½ teaspoon salt and 1 cup water; simmer until water cooks out.

✪ In large serving bowl, combine lettuce, tomatoes, avocado, onions,
olives and pimentos.

✪ When ready to serve, add warm beef mixture, cheese, chips, dressing
and toss. Serve immediately. Serves 8.

Fort Davis National Historic Site is one of the best preserved examples of a frontier military post in the U.S.

★TACO SALAD

1½ pounds lean ground beef
1 onion, chopped
2 teaspoons chili powder
½ teaspoon ground cumin
¾ head lettuce, chopped
3 tomatoes, chopped
1 (16 ounce) package shredded Mexican 4-cheese blend, divided
1 (10 ounce) package original corn chips

✪ In skillet, brown beef and onion; add chili powder and cumin.

✪ When ready to serve, place lettuce, tomatoes and about 8 ounces cheese in large salad bowl. Spoon beef-onion mixture over salad, add remaining cheese and chips and toss. Serve with salsa. Serves 6 to 8.

★LONE STAR CAVIAR

3 (15 ounce) cans black-eyed peas, rinsed, drained
1 (4 ounce) can chopped green chilies, drained
½ purple onion, sliced
2 cups chopped celery
1 sweet red bell pepper, chopped

DRESSING:
⅔ cup white vinegar
⅔ cup sugar
½ cup oil
1 teaspoon seasoned salt
1 teaspoon seasoned pepper
1 teaspoon minced garlic

✪ In bowl, combine peas, green chilies, onion, celery and bell pepper and mix well. In small bowl or jar, combine all dressing ingredients, pour over vegetables and refrigerate. Serves 8.

BLACK-EYED PEA SALAD

2 (15 ounce) can jalapeno black-eyed peas, rinsed, drained
1 ripe avocado, peeled, chopped
½ purple onion, chopped
¾ cup fresh, sliced mushrooms
1 (4 ounce) can chopped green chilies
1 (4 ounce) can chopped ripe olives
1 green bell pepper, seeded, chopped

DRESSING:
⅓ cup oil
⅓ cup white wine vinegar
3 tablespoons sugar
1 tablespoon dried parsley flakes
¼ teaspoon garlic powder
1 teaspoon seasoned salt

✪ In large bowl, mix black-eyed peas, avocado, onions, mushrooms, green chilies, olives and bell pepper.

✪ Mix dressing ingredients, 1 teaspoon salt and ½ teaspoon pepper in small bowl. Add dressing to vegetables, toss and refrigerate. Serves 6 to 8.

GREEN PEA SALAD

1 (16 ounce) package frozen green peas, thawed
1 bunch fresh green onions with tops, chopped
1 red bell pepper, chopped
½ cup chopped celery
½ cup sweet pickle relish
Mayonnaise

✪ Mix all ingredients and use enough mayonnaise to hold salad together. Refrigerate before serving. Serves 6.

 *Editor's Choice*

LAYERED SALAD
This salad makes a beautiful presentation.

½ head lettuce, divided
1 bunch fresh spinach, divided
4 hard-boiled eggs, grated, divided
1 bunch green onions with tops, chopped
1 (15 ounce) can green peas, drained, divided
½ cup chopped celery, divided
½ cup chopped bell pepper, divided
1 cup sliced fresh mushrooms, divided
1 (12 ounce) package shredded cheddar cheese, divided
2 teaspoons sugar, divided
½ cup shredded Monterey Jack cheese

DRESSING:
1½ cups mayonnaise
1½ cups sour cream
1 avocado

✪ Wash, drain and tear lettuce and spinach in pieces.

✪ In large glass bowl, layer half of each of following ingredients: lettuce, spinach, eggs, onions, peas, celery, bell pepper, mushrooms and cheese. Sprinkle with 1 teaspoon sugar, and a little salt and pepper.

✪ In separate bowl mash peeled avocado and mix with mayonnaise and sour cream. Use half the dressing to spread evenly over vegetables.

✪ Repeat layers and sprinkle with remaining teaspoon sugar, and a little salt and pepper. Spread remaining dressing on top.

✪ Spread Monterey Jack cheese over top, cover bowl with plastic wrap and refrigerate overnight. Serves 10.

Simply Scrumptious Shrimp Salad

3 cups cooked chopped shrimp
1 cup chopped celery
4 hard-boiled eggs, chopped
½ cup sliced, green stuffed olives, drained
¼ cup chopped dill pickle
1 cup mayonnaise
2 tablespoons chili sauce
1 tablespoon horseradish
1 teaspoon seasoned salt
¾ teaspoon seasoned pepper

✪ Combine all ingredients, toss lightly and refrigerate. Serve on bed of lettuce. Serves 8.

★Mexicali-Guacamole Salad

5 or 6 avocados
2 green onions with tops, chopped
1 tomato, chopped
3 tablespoons lemon juice
3 tablespoons mayonnaise
1 teaspoon salad oil
4 dashes hot sauce
¼ cup salsa

✪ Chop and partially mash avocados. Mix all ingredients and 2 teaspoons salt.

✪ For salad, serve on bed of chopped lettuce. Serves 6 to 8.

TIP: For dip, serve with chips.

CRUNCHY CAULIFLOWER-BROCCOLI SALAD

1 head cauliflower, cut into florets
1 bunch broccoli, cut into florets
1 cup mayonnaise
¾ cup sour cream
1 tablespoon white wine vinegar
1 tablespoon sugar
½ teaspoon hot sauce
1 onion, chopped

- ✪ After washing cauliflower and broccoli, allow vegetables to rest so they will completely drain.

- ✪ Mix mayonnaise, sour cream, vinegar, sugar, hot sauce, 1 teaspoon salt and ½ teaspoon pepper.

- ✪ Place cauliflower, broccoli and onion in container with lid.

- ✪ Pour dressing over vegetables, toss and refrigerate several hours before serving. Serves 8 to 10.

GARLIC GREEN BEANS

3 (15 ounce) cans whole green beans, drained
⅔ cup oil
½ cup vinegar
½ cup sugar
5 cloves garlic, minced

- ✪ Place green beans in container with lid. Mix oil, vinegar, sugar and garlic and pour over beans. Sprinkle with a little salt and red pepper. Refrigerate over night. Serves 8 to 10.

Texas 1015 SuperSweet Onion Salad

No tears when you peel these onions.

2 large 1015 SuperSweet Onions, sliced
1 (11 ounce) can mandarin oranges, drained, divided
½ cup walnuts, toasted
½ cup crumbled blue cheese
Assorted salad greens
Light vinaigrette dressing

✪ Combine onion and half mandarin oranges. Toss with remaining
   ingredients. Add remaining oranges if needed. Serves 6,

The Texas 1015 SuperSweet Onion is the sweetest onion in the world.

Texas Sweet Onion Stack

2 large Texas Sweet Onions
2 large, garden tomatoes
Olive oil
Fresh lime juice
Chopped basil
Crumbled blue cheese, optional

✪ Cut onions and tomatoes into thick slices and arrange on plate.
   Sprinkle with ½ teaspoon salt and let rest for about 30 minutes.

✪ Drizzle with olive oil and fresh lime juice. Add chopped basil and
   crumbled blue cheese if desired. Serves 4.

TIP: When measuring onions, figure 1 large Texas 1015 SuperSweet Onion
     usually weighs about 1 pound. That is the equivalent of about 5 to 6
     cups onion rings and 2½ cups chopped onions.

IT'S SLAW Y'ALL

1 medium cabbage, finely shredded
1 carrot, grated
1 bunch fresh green onions, chopped
½ cup sour cream
1 cup mayonnaise
1½ tablespoons white vinegar
2½ tablespoons sugar
1 tablespoon poppy seeds

✪ In large bowl, combine cabbage, carrot and green onions.

✪ In small bowl, combine sour cream, mayonnaise, vinegar, sugar and poppy seeds and mix well.   Spoon over vegetables, toss and refrigerate. Searves 4 to 6.

CREAMY CRUNCHY COLE SLAW

4 cups finely shredded cabbage
½ cup minced celery
¼ cup minced bell pepper
1 tablespoon minced green onion
¼ cup sliced pimento, drained
¾ cup sour cream
¼ cup mayonnaise
3 tablespoons vinegar
3 tablespoons sugar
1 teaspoon celery seed

✪ Combine cabbage, celery, bell pepper, onion and pimento.   In separate bowl combine sour cream, mayonnaise, vinegar, sugar, 1 teaspoon salt, ⅛ teaspoon pepper and celery seed, mix well and pour over cabbage.

✪ Mix lightly and refrigerate before serving.   Serves 6.

CORNBREAD SALAD

2 (6 ounce) packages Mexican cornbread mix
2 eggs
1⅓ cups milk
2 ribs celery, sliced
1 bunch green onion with tops, chopped
1 green bell pepper, chopped
2 tomatoes, chopped, drained
8 slices bacon, cooked, crumbled
1 (8 ounce) package shredded cheddar cheese
1 (8 ounce) can whole kernel corn, drained
½ cup ripe chopped olives
2½ cups mayonnaise

✪ Prepare cornbread according to package directions with egg and milk.

✪ Cook, cool and crumble cornbread in large mixing bowl.

✪ Add celery, green onions, bell pepper, tomatoes, bacon, cheese, corn, olives and mayonnaise and toss.

✪ Refrigerate several hours and serve. Serves 8.

Texas has the largest State Fair in the U.S. and the largest ferris wheel in North America.

Big Tex stands at the entrance of the State Fair of Texas and wears the largest pair of jeans in the world. They are Lee Jeans size 276 with a 23-foot waist. His boots are size 70.

BERRY PIZZAZZ

1 (6 ounce) package gelatin
1 (8 ounce) can crushed pineapple with liquid
1 (20 ounce) can blueberry pie filling

TOPPING:
1 (8 ounce) package cream cheese, softened
1 (6 ounce) carton blueberry yogurt
Chopped pecans

✪ Dissolve gelatin in 1 cup boiling water. Add pineapple and fold in blueberry pie filling.

✪ Pour in sprayed 9 x 13-inch glass baking dish, refrigerate until firm.

TOPPING:

✪ Beat cream cheese and yogurt until smooth and spread on gelatin mixture. Garnish with chopped pecans. Serves 8 to 10.

HENNY-PENNY CARROTS

3 (15 ounce) cans cooked, sliced carrots, drained
1 onion, sliced
1 bell pepper, sliced

DRESSING:
1 (10 ounce) can tomato soup
1 teaspoon prepared mustard
1 tablespoon Worcestershire sauce
¾ cup sugar
¼ cup oil
¾ cup vinegar

✪ Combine carrots, onion and bell pepper in bowl with lid.

✪ Mix dressing ingredients and ½ teaspoon salt and pour over vegetables. Cover and refrigerate at least 24 hours before serving.

Encore-Cherry Salad

1 (3 ounce) package raspberry gelatin
1 (20 ounce) can cherry pie filling
1 (3 ounce) package lemon gelatin
1 (3 ounce) package cream cheese, softened
⅓ cup mayonnaise
1 (8 ounce) can crushed pineapple, drained
1 cup whipped topping
Chopped pecans

✪ Dissolve raspberry gelatin in scant 1 cup boiling water and stir in pie filling. Pour in 9 x 13-inch glass dish and refrigerate until set.

✪ Dissolve lemon gelatin in scant 1 cup boiling water.

✪ Beat cream cheese and mayonnaise and gradually add lemon gelatin to mixture. Stir in pineapple and fold in whipped topping.

✪ Pour lemon gelatin mixture over raspberry gelatin mixture, sprinkle pecans over top and refrigerate. Cut into squares to serve. Serves 8 to 10.

Pina Colada Salad

1 (12 ounce) carton small-curd cottage cheese
1 (6 ounce) package lemon gelatin
1 (15 ounce) can crushed pineapple, drained
1 (3½ ounce) can flaked coconut
½ teaspoon coconut extract
½ teaspoon pineapple extract
1 (8 ounce) carton whipped topping

✪ In large mixing bowl, combine cottage cheese and lemon gelatin and mix well.

✪ Add pineapple, coconut and both extracts, fold in whipped topping and refrigerate. Serve in crystal bowl. Serves 8.

Fantastic Fruit Salad

2 (11 ounce) cans mandarin oranges, drained
2 (15 ounce) cans pineapple chunks, drained
1 (16 ounce) carton frozen strawberries, drained
1 (20 ounce) can peach pie filling
1 (20 ounce) can apricot pie filling
2 bananas, sliced

✪ Combine all ingredients, fold gently and refrigerate. Serves 12-16.

TIP: If you want to make a day early, mix oranges, pineapple and pie
fillings and add drained strawberries and bananas at the last minute.

Frozen Holiday Salad

2 (3 ounce) packages cream cheese, softened
2 tablespoons mayonnaise
2 tablespoons sugar
1 (16 ounce) can whole cranberry sauce
1 (8 ounce) can crushed pineapple, drained
½ cup chopped pecans
1 cup miniature marshmallows
1 (8 ounce) carton whipped topping

✪ Beat cream cheese, mayonnaise and sugar to smooth consistency.

✪ Add fruit, pecans and marshmallows and fold in whipped topping.
Pour in sprayed 9 x 13-inch shallow glass dish and freeze.

✪ When ready to serve, take salad out of freezer a few minutes before
cutting in squares. Serves 8 to 10.

BLUE NORTHER STEW

When cold weather comes from the north in Texas, it is called a "norther".

1½ pounds lean ground beef
1 onion, chopped
1 (1 ounce) envelope taco seasoning
1 (1 ounce) envelope ranch dressing mix
1 (15 ounce) can whole kernel corn, drained
1 (15 ounce) can kidney beans with liquid
2 (15 ounce) cans pinto beans
2 (15 ounce) cans Mexican stewed tomatoes
1 (10 ounce) can tomatoes and green chilies
Shredded cheddar or Jack cheese

✪ In large roasting pan, brown ground beef and onion. Add both envelopes seasonings and mix well.

✪ Add corn, beans, stewed tomatoes, tomatoes, green chilies and 1 cup water, mix well and simmer about 30 minutes.

✪ Top each bowl of stew with shredded cheese. Serves 8.

SPICY TURKEY SOUP

3 to 4 cups chopped leftover turkey or chicken
3 (10 ounce) cans chicken broth
2 (10 ounce) cans tomatoes and green chilies
1 (15 ounce) can whole kernel corn
1 large onion, chopped
1 (10 ounce) can condensed tomato soup
1 teaspoon garlic powder
1 teaspoon dried oregano
3 tablespoons cornstarch

✪ In large roasting pan, combine turkey, broth, tomatoes, green chilies, corn, onion, tomato soup, garlic powder and oregano.

✪ Mix cornstarch with 3 tablespoons water and add to soup mixture. Bring to boiling, reduce heat, simmer about 2 hours and stir occasionally. Serves 6 to 8.

SPICY BEAN SOUP

1 cup dried great northern beans
1 ham hock
2 chorizo sausages
1 onion, chopped
½ teaspoon cayenne
1 large potato, cubed
1 bunch turnip greens

✪ Boil beans in 2½ quarts water for 2 minutes. Remove from heat and soak 1 hour.

✪ Add ham hock and bring to boil. Lower heat and simmer for 1½ hours.

✪ Prick sausages with fork and add onion, 2 teaspoons salt, cayenne, potato and sausages. Simmer for 30 minutes.

✪ About 15 minutes before serving, remove sausages and discard. Add finely shredded turnip greens and cook on low for remaining 15 minutes. Serves 6.

Texas had the first rodeo to give prizes in 1883 in the world. It was held in Pecos, Texas with ranch hands from area ranches.

★KITCHEN-SINK TACO SOUP

1¼ pounds lean ground beef
1 onion, chopped
1 (1 ounce) envelope taco seasoning mix
1 (1 ounce) envelope ranch dressing mix
2 (15 ounce) cans pinto beans with liquid
1 (15 ounce) can golden hominy or whole kernel corn with liquid
1 (15 ounce) can cream-style corn
1 (15 ounce) can stewed tomatoes with liquid
1 (15 ounce) can Mexican stewed tomatoes with liquid
1 (8 ounce) package shredded Monterey Jack cheese
Tortilla chips

✪ In skillet, brown ground beef and onion, drain and stir in both seasoning mixes.

✪ In kettle or roasting pan, combine beef-onion mixture, beans, hominy, cream-style corn and both cans stewed tomatoes.

✪ Bring to boil, lower heat and simmer for 10 to 15 minutes. Serve over tortilla chips and sprinkle with cheese. Serves 8 to 10.

Texas held the first indoor rodeo in the world in 1917 in Fort Worth at the Southwestern Exposition and Fat Stock Show.

★TACO SOUP

1½ pounds lean ground beef
1 onion, chopped
1 (1 ounce) package taco seasoning
1 (15 ounce) can whole kernel corn with liquid
1 (15 ounce) can pinto beans with liquid
1 (15 ounce) can Mexican stewed tomatoes with liquid
1 (14 ounce) can beef broth
Sour cream

✪ In large roasting pan, brown beef and chopped onion and stir well.

✪ Add taco seasoning, corn, beans, tomatoes, 1 cup water and broth and stir well.

✪ Bring to boiling point, turn heat down and simmer 2 hours.

✪ Ladle soup in bowls and garnish with dollop of sour cream. Serve with tortilla chips. Serves 8.

EASY POTATO SOUP

1 (16 ounce) package frozen hash brown potatoes
1 cup chopped onion
1 (14 ounce) can chicken broth
1 (14 ounce) can fiesta-nacho soup
1 (14 ounce) can cream of chicken soup
2 cups milk

✪ In large saucepan, combine potatoes, onion and 2 cups water and bring to boil. Cover, reduce heat and simmer 30 minutes.

✪ Stir in broth, soups and milk and heat thoroughly. Serves 6 to 8.

Wild West Soup

1 cup wild rice
3 ribs celery, diced
1 onion, chopped
½ sweet red bell pepper, diced
½ green bell pepper, diced
½ cup (1 stick) butter
½ cup flour
1 teaspoon seasoned salt
⅛ teaspoon cayenne pepper
3 (14 ounce) cans chicken broth
1 (16 ounce) carton half-and-half cream
¼ cup white wine

✪ Cook rice according to package directions.

✪ In skillet, saute celery, onion and bell peppers in butter just until tender-crisp. Sprinkle with flour, seasoned salt, ½ teaspoon pepper and cayenne pepper and stir to blend, but not brown.

✪ On low heat, add chicken broth and rice and cook until mixture thickens slightly, stirring constantly. When ready to serve, stir in cream and white wine. Serves 6 to 8.

The cities of El Paso and Ciudad Juarez form the second largest bi-national population in the world.

White Lightning Bean Stew

1½ cups dried navy beans
3 (14 ounce) cans chicken broth
¼ cup (½ stick) butter
1 onion, chopped
1 clove garlic, minced
3 cups chopped, cooked chicken
1 (4 ounce) can chopped green chilies
½ teaspoon sweet basil
1½ teaspoons ground cumin
½ teaspoon dried oregano
⅛ teaspoon cayenne pepper
⅛ teaspoon ground cloves
Shredded Monterey Jack cheese

✪ Sort, wash beans and place in kettle. Cover with water 2 inches above beans and soak overnight.

✪ Drain beans and add broth, butter, 1 cup water, onion and garlic. Bring to boil, reduce heat and cover. Simmer 2 hours, stirring occasionally, and add water if needed.

✪ With potato masher, mash half the beans several times. Add chicken, green chilies, ½ teaspoon pepper and seasonings. Bring to boil, reduce heat and cover. Simmer another 30 minutes.

✪ When ready to serve, spoon in bowls and top with 1 to 2 tablespoons cheese. Serves 8.

★TORTILLA SOUP

1 onion, chopped
1 small green bell pepper, chopped
1 teaspoon minced garlic
2 tablespoons oil
2 (14 ounce) cans chicken broth
1 (14 ounce) can beef broth
1 (6 ounce) can tomato paste
1 (4 ounce) can chopped green chilies
1 (15 ounce) can stewed tomatoes
1 teaspoon chili powder
1 teaspoon ground cumin
1 tablespoon dried parsley flakes
1 tablespoon Worcestershire sauce
1 cup finely chopped, cooked chicken breast
8 (8 inch) corn tortillas
1 cup shredded Monterey Jack cheese

✪ In skillet, saute onion, bell pepper and garlic in oil. Transfer to large roasting pan and add chicken broth, beef broth, tomato paste, green chilies, stewed tomatoes, all seasonings, and 1 teaspoon each of salt and pepper.

✪ Cover and simmer for 1 hour. Add chicken and simmer another 5 minutes. Cut tortillas in narrow strips and fry until crisp.

✪ When ready to serve, place a few crisp tortilla strips in soup bowls, fill with soup and sprinkle heaping tablespoon cheese and more crisp tortilla strips on top. Serves 8.

★TOMATO-TORTILLA SOUP

8 corn tortillas, cut into strips
Hot oil for frying
1 onion, chopped
½ cup finely chopped green bell pepper
½ teaspoon ground cumin
2 teaspoons minced garlic
2 tablespoons oil
2 (15 ounce) cans diced tomatoes
1 (4 ounce) can chopped green chilies
3 (14 ounce) cans chicken broth
½ bunch fresh cilantro, very finely chopped
1 (8 ounce) package shredded cheddar cheese
2 cups chopped, cooked chicken breasts, optional

✪ Fry tortilla strips in hot oil and drain on paper towels.

✪ In large kettle or heavy pot, saute onion, bell pepper, cumin and garlic in 2 tablespoons oil.

✪ Add diced tomatoes, green chilies, chicken broth, cilantro and chicken and stir occasionally. Cook for 20 to 25 minutes.

✪ When ready to serve, place some tortilla strips and shredded cheese in each bowl, pour soup into bowls and serve immediately. Serves 8.

The largest petroleum refinery in the U.S. began in 1919 by the Humble Oil Company. Humble was the first gasoline company to issue credit cards. In 1973 the Humble Oil Company became Exxon Company, USA.

Editor's Choice

Incredible Broccoli-Cheese Soup

1 (10 ounce) box frozen chopped broccoli
3 tablespoons butter
½ onion, finely chopped
¼ cup flour
1 (16 ounce) carton half-and-half
1 (14 ounce) can chicken broth
⅛ teaspoon cayenne pepper
½ teaspoon summer savory
1 (16 ounce) package cubed, mild Mexican Velveeta®

❂ Punch several holes in box of broccoli and microwave on high 5 minutes. Rotate box in microwave and cook on high another 4 minutes. Leave in microwave for 3 minutes.

❂ In large saucepan, melt butter and cook onion until it is translucent. Add flour, stir and gradually add half-and-half, chicken broth, ½ teaspoon salt, ¼ teaspoon pepper and seasonings and stir constantly.

❂ Heat until mixture thickens. (Do not boil.) Add cheese and stir constantly until cheese melts. Add cooked broccoli and serve hot. Serves 6.

Texas has the largest road system of any state in the U.S. There are 79,535 center-line miles.

The longest highway in one state is US 83 that runs from Brownsville to the Panhandle for 903 miles. The second longest highway is IH-10 that runs from El Paso to east of Orange pooooo for 878 miles.

The world's largest parking lot is at DFW Airport.

PANCHO VILLA STEW

3 cups diced, cooked ham
1 pound smoked sausage, cut in ½-inch slices
3 (14 ounce) cans chicken broth
2 (15 ounce) cans Mexican stewed tomatoes
1 onion, chopped
1 teaspoon minced garlic
2 teaspoons ground cumin
2 teaspoons cocoa
1 teaspoon dried oregano
2 (15 ounce) cans pinto beans with liquid
1 (15 ounce) can yellow hominy with liquid
1 (8 ounce) can whole kernel corn
Flour tortillas

✪ In large roasting pan or kettle, combine ham, sausage, broth, tomatoes, onion, garlic, cumin, cocoa, oregano and 1 teaspoon salt, mix well and bring to boil. Reduce heat and simmer for 45 minutes.

✪ Add beans, hominy and corn and simmer another 15 minutes. Serve with warm, buttered flour tortillas. Serves 8.

AVOCADO-CREAM SOUP

4 ripe avocados, peeled, diced
1½ cups whipping cream
2 (14 ounce) cans chicken broth
¼ cup dry sherry

✪ Blend half avocados and half cream. Repeat with remaining avocados and cream. Bring broth to boil, reduce heat and stir in avocado puree. Add 1 teaspoon salt and sherry and refrigerate thoroughly. Serves 6.

★MENUDO

This could also be called "Mexican Hangover Helper" or at least it is reported to be a sure cure for "the morning after".

2 pounds tripe
1 bunch green onions with tops, chopped
3 cloves garlic, minced
¾ cup snipped fresh cilantro leaves, divided
Fresh lime slices

✪ Wash tripe very well and dry with paper towels. Place tripe in large Dutch oven or stew pot with enough water to cover plus 3 inches.

✪ Add onions and garlic, bring to boil, reduce heat and simmer 6 to 8 hours until tripe is tender. Add water if necessary.

✪ When tripe is tender, remove from pot and cool about 15 minutes. Cut into small pieces and return to stew pot.

✪ Add ¼ cup cilantro and cook another 1 to 2 hours.

✪ Serve in large soup bowls and garnish with remaining cilantro and lime slices. Serves 6 to 8.

TIP: Menudo or tripe soup is a favorite in Mexico and has been part of the Texas cattle culture since cattle-drive days. Tripe is the inner lining of beef stomach and is very tough, requiring long cooking times.

Slim's Tidbit:

"After ya eat Menudo and Calf Fries, nobody can call ya a gringo. Ya can ride tha range with tha best of 'em.

BEANS

One of the basic food groups in Texas is beans, but it refers almost exclusively to pinto beans and black-eyed peas. When Texans talk about a pot of beans, it is a pot of pinto beans with ham hock, salt pork or bacon and jalapenos on the side. When Texans want good luck in the New Year, they always eat black-eyed peas. Black-eyed peas are especially good with ham and cornbread.

 *Slim's Tidbit:*

"In Texas when ya talk about frijoles or beans, you're talkin' pinto beans. Not green 'uns or red 'uns or anythang else. We call 'em whistleberries. We like 'um, even tho' they talk behind ya back sometimes."

 *Editor's Choice*

★BEST LITTLE BEANS IN TEXAS

3 cups dried pinto beans
½ pound salt pork or ham hock
2 to 3 jalapeno peppers, chopped
1 onion, chopped
2 tablespoons chili powder
1 teaspoon garlic powder
1 teaspoon oregano

✪ Wash beans, cover with water and soak overnight.

✪ Drain beans and cover again with water. Add all ingredients.

✪ Bring to boil. Reduce heat and simmer in covered pot about 3 hours or until beans are tender. (Add water if needed.) Serves 10 to 14.

TIP: Before serving, add salt only if seasoning with ham.

★PECOS WHISTLEBERRIES

3 cups dry pinto beans, washed
2 tablespoons chili powder
1 jalapeno pepper, cut in wedges
¼ cup onion, chopped
2 teaspoons garlic powder
½ teaspoon ground cumin
2 tablespoons cilantro
3 tablespoons ketchup
¼ cup (½ stick) butter

✪ Place beans in 8-quart saucepan, pour 5 quarts boiling water over beans and soak overnight.

✪ Cook on high uncovered for 30 minutes. Lower heat and add all ingredients.

✪ Cover and simmer for 2½ to 3 hours or until beans are soft. Add about 1 teaspoon salt before serving. Serve hot with flour tortillas and jalapenos. Serves 14 to 16.

★FRIJOLES REFRITOS

Refried Beans. These are just recycled pinto beans with some other stuff in 'em.

Leftover, cooked pinto beans
Bacon drippings
Shredded cheddar cheese

✪ Cook leftover beans until most or all of liquid is gone. Drain any excess liquid and mash remaining beans.

✪ In large, heavy skillet with bacon drippings, fry mashed beans until they are thoroughly heated and mixed with bacon drippings.

✪ Serve immediately with cheese on top.

★FRIJOLES CON JAMON
Beans with ham

2 cups dried pinto beans
1 cup chopped ham
4 to 6 jalapenos, stemmed, seeded, minced
2 onions, chopped
3 tomatoes, chopped
2 teaspoons Worcestershire sauce

✪ Sort pinto beans, rinse and soak overnight in enough water to cover. When ready to cook, drain beans, add ham and pour in 6 cups water.

✪ Bring to boil, reduce heat and add jalapenos, onion, tomatoes and Worcestershire. Simmer for 2 to 3 hours or until beans are almost tender.

✪ Taste to adjust seasonings and add salt and pepper as needed.

✪ Simmer 30 to 45 minutes to blend flavors and serve. Serves 8 to 12.

Slim's Tidbit:
"Real Texicans eat frijoles. Gringos eat beans."

M ore jalapenos are eaten in Texas than in any other state in the U.S.

★FRIJOLES RANCHERO

Pinto beans are the beans real cowboys ate and still eat, along with a "couple a hunard million" other Texans. The real beans always have ham hock, salt pork or bacon.

1 pound pinto beans
¾ pound salt pork, ham or bacon
1 onion, chopped
2 teaspoons minced garlic
1 small green bell pepper, finely chopped
1 (15 ounce) can diced tomatoes
1 (15 ounce) can enchilada sauce
1 teaspoon ground cumin

✪ Place beans in saucepan and cover with boiling water. Soak for 30 minutes to 1 hour.

✪ Place salt pork in large saucepan with about 3 cups water, bring to boiling, lower heat and simmer for 30 minutes.

✪ Add drained beans to salt pork and simmer for about 2 hours or until beans are tender.

✪ Add onion, garlic, bell pepper, tomatoes, enchilada sauce and cumin and continue cooking on low heat for 1 more hour. Check several times to see if more water is needed. Serves 8 to 12.

In the 1880's on one day in Fort Worth, more than 200,000 buffalo hides were sold. Had it not been for the efforts of Texas Ranger Col. Charles Goodnight to control hunting, the buffalo might be extinct today.

TRAIL DRIVE WHISTLERS

2 pounds dried pinto beans
1 medium piece salt pork
5 slices uncooked bacon, chopped
2 (10 ounce) cans tomatoes and green chilies
1 onion, chopped
¼ teaspoon ground oregano
½ teaspoon ground cumin
2 teaspoons minced garlic

✪ Place pinto beans in large saucepan. Rinse and cover with water. Soak overnight or at least 3 hours. Drain and cover with fresh water.

✪ Add salt pork, bacon, tomatoes, green chilies and onion. Bring to a boil, add more water if needed, lower heat and simmer for 3 hours or until beans are tender.

✪ Add oregano, cumin, garlic and ½ teaspoon salt in the last 30 minutes of cooking. Serves 10 to 14.

Slim's Tidbit:

"Cowboys ate a lot a pinto beans on tha trail 'cause they were easy to git and easy enough to carry. They liked 'em cause they said they'd stick to your ribs."

BRAZOS BAKED BEANS

½ pound bacon
2 onions, chopped
1 green bell pepper, chopped
2 (28 ounce) cans pork and beans with liquid
1 cup chili sauce
2 cups packed brown sugar
¼ teaspoon dry mustard
1 teaspoon minced garlic
¼ cup Worcestershire sauce
2 teaspoons liquid smoke

✪ Preheat oven to 350°. In skillet, fry bacon, remove from skillet and crumble. Add onions and bell pepper to skillet with remaining bacon drippings; cook until onions and bell peppers are tender. Add all remaining ingredients and mix well.

✪ Pour into sprayed 3-quart baking dish and bake covered for 30 minutes. Reduce oven to 300° and cook another 90 minutes. Serves 8 to 10.

TEXOMA BAKED BEANS

2 (15 ounce) cans pork and beans, slightly drained
1 tablespoon Worcestershire sauce
½ onion, chopped
⅔ cup packed brown sugar
3 dashes hot sauce
1 teaspoon prepared mustard
¼ cup ketchup
3 strips bacon

✪ Preheat oven to 350°. In mixing bowl, combine beans, Worcestershire, onion, sugar, hot sauce, mustard and ketchup and mix well.

✪ Pour into sprayed casserole dish and place bacon strips over beans. Bake for 45 to 50 minutes. Serves 6.

HOME-ON-THE-RANGE STEW

1½ pounds lean stew meat
2 tablespoons oil
2 (14 ounce) cans beef broth
2 large onions, chopped
1 teaspoon minced garlic
3 ribs celery, sliced in 1-inch pieces
2 carrots, sliced in 1-inch pieces
1 green bell pepper
2 potatoes, cubed
2 (15 ounce) cans whole tomatoes
2 (10 ounce) cans tomatoes and green chilies
2 (15 ounce) cans black beans, rinsed, drained
1 (15 ounce) can yellow hominy
2 tablespoons chili powder
½ teaspoon oregano powder
1 teaspoon ground cumin
2 serrano peppers, sliced
2 (15 ounce) cans Spanish rice

✪ In large skillet, brown and cook stew meat in oil for about 10 minutes. Transfer meat to stew pot. (Cubed left-over beef roast may also be used.)

✪ Add beef broth, onions, garlic, celery, carrots bell pepper and potatoes. Bring to boiling point, reduce heat and simmer for 30 minutes or until carrots and potatoes are tender.

✪ Add tomatoes, tomatoes and green chilies, black beans, hominy, chili powder, oregano powder, cumin, ½ teaspoon salt and serrano peppers and heat.

✪ When ready to serve, heat Spanish rice in saucepan and place a layer of rice in bottom of individual bowls and spoon stew over rice. (Plain cooked white rice could also be used.) Garnish with chopped green onions if you have them. Serves 10 to 12.

★SMOKED JALAPENOS

As the head honcho of the pepper world, jalapenos are a side dish in Texas.

10 to 12 jalapenos
3 to 4 cloves garlic, minced
¼ to ½ cup (½ to 1 stick) butter
2 tablespoons liquid smoke

✪ Slice jalapenos in half and remove seeds. Spread butter on each half and sprinkle minced garlic over each half.

✪ Place jalapenos on heavy foil. Sprinkle liquid smoke over jalapenos and wrap tightly.

✪ Place foil package over charcoal fire and cook for about 1 hour, if jalapenos are medium to large. Serves 8 to 10.

———◆———

FRIED JALAPENOS

1 (14 ounce) can whole pickled jalapenos
1 (8 ounce) package shredded cheddar cheese
2 eggs
½ cup milk
¾ cup flour
Oil

✪ Cut tops off jalapenos and seed. Stuff about 1 tablespoon cheese inside each jalapeno. In bowl, combine eggs and milk. In separate bowl, stir flour with a little salt and pepper.

✪ Roll filled jalapenos in flour mixture, then in egg mixture and again in flour. Line jalapenos on baking sheet and fry in hot oil about 350° until golden brown. Serves 5 to 6.

———◆———

★TEXAS BLACK-EYED PEAS

It is a Texas tradition to eat black-eyed peas on New Year's day for good luck.

1 bell pepper, chopped
1 large onion, chopped
2 ribs celery, chopped
2 tablespoons (¼ stick) butter
2 (15 ounce) cans jalapeno black-eyed peas
1 (15 ounce) can stewed tomatoes
1 teaspoon garlic powder
¼ cup ketchup
3 chicken bouillon cubes

✪ Saute bell pepper, onion and celery in butter until crisp-tender.

✪ Add remaining ingredients and simmer 10 minutes. Serves 8 to 10.

TIP: **Serve this with cornbread and you will get praises from everyone who likes black-eyed peas.**

Slim's Tidbit:

"What most people call black-eyed peas, cowboys call 'cowpeas'. I guess 'cause they used to feed 'em to tha animals. I heard 'bout an ol' chuck wagon cook who ran out a frijoles on tha trail down by tha Pecos. Now, that's a real bad thang. He cooked up a batch of those cowpeas, put a big ol' slab a bacon in 'em and got a real good scald on 'em. Those boys liked 'em just fine. Turned out ta be tha best darn trail drive in a month of Sund'ys. Those ol' cowboys decided it must a been tha cowpeas that brought 'em good luck and that's why Texans eat cowpeas for good luck! I got a bunch of these true, Texas stories in my gourd. How much time ya got?"

A thens, Texas is called the Black-Eyed Pea Capital of the World.

BAKED SQUASH OLÉ

4 to 5 cups cooked squash, drained
1 onion, chopped
1 (4 ounce) can chopped green chilies, drained
¾ cup shredded Monterey Jack cheese
1 (10¾ ounce) can cream of chicken soup
1 cup sour cream
½ cup (1 stick) butter, melted
1 package herb dressing mix

✪ Preheat oven to 375°.

✪ Place cooked squash in a mixing bowl and add 1 teaspoon salt, ½ teaspoon pepper, onion, green chilies, cheese, soup and sour cream. Mix well.

✪ Mix butter and herb dressing mix. Place one-half herb dressing mixture in a sprayed 9 x 13-inch baking dish. Pour squash mixture on top. Sprinkle with remaining herb dressing mixture. Bake for 30 minutes. Serves 10.

GREEN PEAS WITH WATER CHESTNUTS

2 (10 ounce) packages frozen green peas
1 (8 ounce) can sliced water chestnuts, drained, chopped
1 (10 ounce) can cream of mushroom soup

✪ Preheat oven to 350°.

✪ Prepare green peas according to package directions and drain.

✪ Stir in water chestnuts and soup. Heat well in saucepan or pour into sprayed baking dish and bake for 25 minutes. Serves 6.

SOUTH TEXAS BLACK-EYED PEAS

¾ pound bacon, cut into small pieces
2 (16 ounce) packages frozen shelled black-eyed peas, thawed
2 jalapenos, seeded, chopped
½ green bell pepper, chopped
1 onion, chopped
2 ribs celery, sliced
1 teaspoon sugar
½ teaspoon seasoned salt

✪ Combine all ingredients and 1 teaspoon each of salt and pepper in large saucepan with 1 quart water and bring to boil.

✪ Reduce heat to low, cover and simmer for about 2 hours or until peas are tender. Serves 8 to 10.

GRILLED CORN-ON-THE-COB

Native Texans call corn-on-the-cob "sweet corn" or "roastin ears".

Fresh corn-on-the-cob in husks
Butter

✪ Shuck each ear of corn by removing outer husks, but save larger husks.

✪ Remove all silks on corn and spread butter all over corn. Season with salt and pepper and wrap corn in inner husks and large outer husks to hold butter. Tie with long pieces of outer husks.

✪ Place on grill and cook 15 to 30 minutes, depending on coals and size of corn. Turn once or twice while cooking. Remove from grill and serve hot.

JALAPENO GREEN BEANS

1 (8 ounce) carton sour cream
1 (8 ounce) package jalapeno Velveeta® cheese, cubed
1 onion, finely minced
3 (15 ounce) cans green beans, drained
2 cups crushed crispy rice cereal or corn flakes
2 tablespoons (¼ stick) butter, melted

✪ Preheat oven to 350°.

✪ In large saucepan on low heat, melt sour cream and Velveeta cheese and stir constantly.

✪ Add onion and green beans and mix well.

✪ Pour in sprayed 9 x 13-inch baking dish.

✪ Combine crushed crispy rice cereal and butter, sprinkle over green bean mixture and bake for 35 minutes. Serves 8 to 10.

HOTTER 'N HELL GREEN BEANS

3 (15 ounce) cans green beans, drained
1 (8 ounce) can sliced water chestnuts, drained, chopped
1 (16 ounce) packages shredded Mexican Velveeta® cheese
1 cup cracker crumbs
2 (5 ounce) cans onion rings

✪ Preheat oven to 350°.

✪ Place green beans in 9 x 13-inch baking dish and cover with water chestnuts.

✪ Sprinkle cheese over top and cracker crumbs over cheese.

✪ Arrange onion rings over casserole and bake for 25 to 30 minutes. Serves 10.

GREEN BEAN SUPREME

2 tablespoons (¼ stick) butter
1 (10 ounce) can cream of mushroom soup
1 (3 ounce) package cream cheese, softened
3 (15 ounce) cans French-style green beans, drained
1 tablespoon dried onion flakes
1 (8 ounce) can sliced water chestnuts, drained
½ teaspoon garlic powder
½ teaspoon seasoned salt
1 (12 ounce) package shredded cheddar cheese
1 cup cracker crumbs
1 (2 ounce) package slivered almonds

✪ Preheat oven to 350°.

✪ Melt butter in large saucepan and add soup and cream cheese. Cook over low heat, stirring constantly just until cream cheese melts and mixture is fairly smooth.

✪ Remove from heat, stir in green beans, onion flakes, water chestnuts, garlic powder, seasoned salt and cheese and mix well.

✪ Pour into sprayed 9 x 13-inch casserole dish. Top with cracker crumbs and then almonds.

✪ Bake uncovered for 30 minutes or until casserole bubbles around edges. Serves 8 to 10.

Slim's Tidbit:
*"This green bean deal's been around for as long as
I can remember, but I shore do like 'em."*

ALMOND-ASPARAGUS BAKE

A family favorite

5 (10.5 ounce) cans asparagus, drained, divided
1½ cups cracker crumbs, divided
4 eggs, hard-boiled, sliced, divided
1 (12 ounce) package shredded cheddar cheese, divided
½ cup (1 stick) butter, melted
½ cup milk
1 (2.3 ounce) package sliced almonds

✪ Preheat oven to 350°.

✪ Arrange half asparagus in sprayed 9 x 13-inch baking dish.

✪ Cover with ¾ cup cracker crumbs and half sliced eggs and sprinkle with half cheese.

✪ Layer remaining asparagus, remaining eggs and ¾ cup cracker crumbs.

✪ Drizzle butter and milk over casserole and top with almonds and remaining cheese. Bake for 30 minutes. Serves 8.

CORN-GREEN CHILE CASSEROLE

2 (10 ounce) packages frozen whole kernel corn
2 tablespoons butter
1 (8 ounce) package cream cheese
1 tablespoon sugar
1 (4 ounce) can chopped green chilies

✪ Preheat oven to 350°.

✪ Cook corn according to package directions, drain and set aside. Melt butter in saucepan over low heat, add cream cheese and stir until it melts.

✪ Stir in corn, sugar and green chilies. Pour into 2-quart baking dish. Cover and bake for 25 minutes. Serves 6.

SOMBRERO-CORN CASSEROLE

1 (15 ounce) can cream-style corn
1 (8 ounce) can whole kernel corn, drained
1 cup biscuit mix
1 egg, beaten
¼ cup oil
½ cup milk
1 (7 ounce) can chopped green chilies, drained
1 (8 ounce) package shredded 4-cheese blend, divided

✪ Preheat oven to 375°.

✪ In bowl, combine both cans corn, biscuit mix, egg, oil and milk.

✪ Spread half of mixture in sprayed 7 x 11-inch baking dish.

✪ Cover with chopped green chilies and three-fourths cheese. Spread remaining batter over top.

✪ Bake covered for 30 minutes. Remove from oven, sprinkle remaining cheese over top and return to oven for 5 minutes. Serves 6 to 8.

MAMA'S CORN FRITTERS

3 teaspoons baking powder
1½ cups flour
½ teaspoon sugar
1 egg, beaten
1 (8 ounce) can whole kernel corn, drained
Milk
Oil for frying

✪ Sift dry ingredients and ½ teaspoon salt. Add egg, corn and only enough milk to make batter consistency.

✪ Mix well and drop batter by tablespoons in hot oil and fry until golden brown. Yield: About 2 dozen fritters.

 *Editor's Choice*

CORNBREAD DRESSING AND GRAVY

The best dressing in the world!

2 (6 ounce) packages cornbread mix
9 biscuits or 1 recipe of biscuit mix
1 small onion, chopped
2 ribs celery, chopped
2 eggs
2 teaspoons poultry seasoning
3 (14 ounce) cans chicken broth, divided

GRAVY:
2 (14 ounce) cans chicken broth
2 heaping tablespoons cornstarch
2 hard-boiled eggs, sliced, optional

✪ Several days ahead of time prepare cornbread and biscuits according to package instructions.

✪ Preheat oven to 350º.

✪ Crumble cornbread and biscuits into large bowl, using a little more cornbread than biscuits.

✪ Add onion, celery, eggs, poultry seasoning and a little pepper. Stir in 2½ cans chicken broth. (If the mixture is not "runny", add remaining broth. If it is still not runny, add a little milk.)

✪ Bake in sprayed 9 x 13-inch glass baking dish for about 45 minutes or until golden brown. This may be frozen uncooked, thawed and cooked when you want it.

GRAVY:

✪ Mix cornstarch with ½ cup broth in saucepan and mix until there are no lumps.

✪ Add remaining broth and heat to boiling, stirring constantly, until broth thickens.

✪ Add hard-boiled eggs and a little pepper and pour into a gravy bowl. Serves 8 to 10.

YUMMY YELLOW SQUASH

4 cups cooked yellow squash, drained
1 (2 ounce) jar diced pimento, drained
1 carrot, grated
1 (8 ounce) can sliced water chestnuts, drained
1 cup sour cream
1 cup cottage cheese, drained
1 (3 ounce) package cream cheese, softened
1 (12 ounce) package shredded Monterey Jack cheese
¼ cup (½ stick) butter, melted
1 (16 ounce) package chicken stuffing mix

✪ Preheat oven to 350°.

✪ After squash drains, add pimento, carrot and water chestnuts and mix well.

✪ In another bowl mix sour cream, cottage cheese, cream cheese, Jack cheese and butter and mix well. Stir in half stuffing mix and all seasoning with stuffing; fold in squash.

✪ Spoon in lightly sprayed 3-quart casserole and sprinkle remaining stuffing mix over top. Bake for 30 to 35 minutes. Serves 8 to 10.

CHILE-CHEESE SQUASH

1 pound yellow squash, diced
⅔ cup mayonnaise
1 (4 ounce) can diced green chilies, drained
⅔ cup shredded longhorn cheese
⅔ cup breadcrumbs

✪ Cook squash in salted water just until tender-crisp and drain. Return to saucepan, stir in mayonnaise, chilies, cheese and breadcrumbs. Serve hot. Serves 6.

GRINGO ZUCCHINI

4 eggs
1 (8 ounce) package shredded Monterey Jack cheese
1 (8 ounce) package shredded Mexican 4-cheese blend
1 cup grated zucchini
1 (4 ounce) can chopped green chilies
1 (2 ounce) jar sliced pimentos, drained
1 onion, finely chopped
1 teaspoon seasoned salt
⅛ teaspoon cayenne pepper
1 cup crushed croutons
⅓ cup grated parmesan cheese

✪ Preheat oven to 350°.

✪ In large mixing bowl, beat eggs well. Stir in both cheeses, zucchini, green chilies, pimentos, onion, seasoned salt and cayenne pepper and mix well.

✪ Pour into well sprayed 2-quart baking dish. Mix croutons and parmesan cheese and sprinkle over top.

✪ Bake uncovered for 35 minutes. Serves 8.

SEASONED SQUASH AND ONIONS

8 zucchini, sliced
2 onions, chopped
¼ cup (½ stick) butter
1 (10 ounce) can fiesta-nacho cheese soup
1 (6 ounce) can french-fried onion rings

✪ Cook squash and onion in small amount of water until tender and drain. Add butter, soup and onion rings and toss. Serve hot. Serves 6.

CREAM-STYLE ZUCCHINI

5 large zucchini, sliced
½ onion, chopped
1 (15 ounce) can cream-style corn
1 (8 ounce) package cream cheese, softened
1 tablespoon cornstarch
1 (4 ounce) can chopped green chilies, drained
½ teaspoon seasoned pepper
1½ cups cracker crumbs

✪ Preheat oven to 350°.

✪ Cook squash and onion in boiling water just until tender-crisp and drain well.

✪ Add corn, cream cheese and cornstarch, leave on low burner and stir until cream cheese melts.

✪ Stir in green chilies, 1 teaspoon salt and seasoned pepper. Pour in large casserole dish and top with cracker crumbs.

✪ Bake for 45 minutes. Serves 8 to 10.

FRIED YELLOW SQUASH OR ZUCCHINI

2 large yellow squash or zucchini, sliced
1 egg, beaten
2 tablespoons milk
¾ cup cornmeal
¾ cup flour
Oil

✪ Place squash on plate and sprinkle with a little salt and pepper. Combine eggs and milk in a small bowl. In separate shallow bowl, combine cornmeal and flour.

✪ Dip squash slices in egg-milk mixture and then in cornmeal-flour mixture. Fry in skillet in a little hot oil. Drain on paper towel. Serves 4 to 6.

FREDRICKSBURG SWEET-SOUR CABBAGE

4 slices bacon, cut in small pieces
1 medium head cabbage
½ onion, diced
1 apple, diced
1 tablespoon vinegar
1 tablespoon sugar
1½ tablespoons flour, optional

✪ In large skillet, fry bacon and drain on paper towels.

✪ With bacon drippings still in skillet, cut cabbage very, very fine and add to hot fat. Add onion and apple and stir well.

✪ Add 2 cups water and cook on low heat 1 hour. (Liquid should cook down in this time.)

✪ Season with a little salt and pepper, vinegar, and sugar. If desired, thicken by mixing flour with a little warm water and stir it into dish. Serves 4.

The largest natural gas field in the world is located north of Amarillo and is called Panhandle-Hugoton Field. It is estimated that the field contains more than 25 trillion cubic feet of gas and has produced over 8 trillion since its discovery in 1918.

CAULIFLOWER CON QUESO

1 large cauliflower, broken in flowerets
¼ cup (½ stick) butter
¼ cup chopped onion
2 tablespoons flour
1 (15 ounce) can stewed tomatoes
1 (4 ounce) can chopped green chilies, drained
¾ teaspoon seasoned pepper
¼ teaspoon hot sauce
1 (8 ounce) package shredded Monterey Jack cheese

✪ Cook flowerets until just crisp-tender. Drain and set aside.

✪ Melt butter in medium saucepan. Add onion and cook until clear.

✪ Blend in flour, then stir in tomatoes. Cook, stirring constantly, until mixture thickens.

✪ Add green chilies, seasoned pepper, 1 teaspoon salt and hot sauce, fold in cheese and stir until cheese melts.

✪ Pour sauce over drained hot cauliflower and serve. Serves 6.

Texas has 6 very different, very distinct geographical areas.
1. Desert plains of the Texas Panhandle
2. Blackland prairies of North Texas
3. Piney wood forests of East Texas
4. Coastal wetlands and beaches of the Gulf Coast
5. Rolling hills and lakes of the Hill Country
6. Desert mountains and deep canyons of the Big Bend and Guadalupe Mountains.

PECAN-BROCCOLI BAKE

2 (16 ounce) packages frozen chopped broccoli
1 (10 ounce) can cream of chicken soup
1 (10 ounce) can cream of celery soup
1¼ cups mayonnaise
3 eggs, well beaten
1 onion, chopped
1 cup chopped pecans
2 cups seasoned breadcrumbs
¼ cup (½ stick) butter, melted
1 (8 ounce) package shredded cheddar cheese, optional

✪ Preheat oven to 350°.

✪ Cook broccoli according to package directions, drain well and place in large mixing bowl.

✪ Add chicken soup, celery soup, mayonnaise, eggs, onion and pecans. Spoon into sprayed 9 x 13-inch casserole dish.

✪ Toss breadcrumbs with melted butter and sprinkle over top of casserole.

✪ Bake uncovered for 25 minutes. Sprinkle cheese over top and return to oven for 5 minutes. Serves 8 to 10.

There are four national forests in the eastern part of Texas: Angelina National Forest, Sam Houston National Forest, Davy Crockett National Forest and Sabine National Forest.

Padre Island National Seashore with more than 70 miles of seashore is the longest undeveloped barrier island in the U.S.

SPICY BROCCOLI-RICE WHIZ

1¼ cups rice
¾ cup chopped onion
¾ cup chopped bell pepper
¾ cup chopped celery
¼ cup (½ stick) butter
1 (8 ounce) package cubed Mexican Velveeta® cheese
1 (10 ounce) can cream of chicken soup
½ cup milk
1 (16 ounce) package frozen chopped broccoli, thawed

✪ Preheat oven to 350°.

✪ Cook rice in large saucepan and drain. Saute onions, bell pepper and celery in butter.

✪ Add onion, bell pepper and celery to rice while hot. Fold in Velveeta cheese, chicken soup and milk and mix. Heat on low burner just until cheese and soup blend well. Fold in chopped broccoli.

✪ Pour in sprayed, 3-quart baking dish, cover and bake for 30 to 35 minutes. Serves 8 to 10.

TIP: This may be made 1 day ahead, refrigerateed and baked the following day.

The Texas State Capitol in Austin is 7 feet taller than the U.S. Capitol in Washington, D.C.

Editor's Choice

SPINACH ENCHILADAS

2 (10 ounce) packages chopped spinach, thawed, drained well
1 (1 ounce) envelope dry onion soup mix
1 (12 ounce) package shredded cheddar cheese, divided
1 (12 ounce) package Monterey Jack cheese, divided
12 flour tortillas
1 pint whipping cream

✪ Preheat oven to 350°.

✪ Squeeze spinach between paper towels to completely remove excess
moisture. In medium bowl, combine spinach and onion soup mix.
Blend in half cheddar cheese and half Monterey Jack cheese.

✪ Lay out 12 tortillas, place about 3 heaping tablespoons spinach
mixture down middle of tortilla and roll up tortillas.

✪ Place each filled tortilla, seam side down, in sprayed 10 x 15-inch
baking dish.

✪ Pour cream over enchiladas and sprinkle with remaining cheese.

✪ Bake covered for 15 minutes. Uncover and bake for another
15 minutes. Cool slightly and use spatula to serve enchiladas.
Serves 10 - 12.

TIP: This recipe freezes well. To make ahead of time, freeze before adding
the cream and remaining cheese. Thaw in the refrigerator the night
before cooking. These are so good and so much fun to make and serve!
Eat them all because the tortillas get a little tough if reheated.

EASY CHEESY SPINACH

2 (10 ounce) packages frozen, chopped spinach
2 cups cottage cheese
2½ cups shredded sharp cheddar cheese
4 eggs, beaten
3 tablespoons flour
¼ cup (½ stick) butter, melted
¼ teaspoon garlic salt
½ teaspoon lemon pepper
¼ teaspoon celery salt
1 teaspoon minced onion

✪ Preheat oven to 325°.

✪ Drain spinach thoroughly and press between paper towels to remove excess liquid.

✪ Mix spinach with remaining ingredients and place in sprayed 3-quart casserole. Bake for 1 hour. Serves 8.

TIP: Casserole may be made a day ahead and baked when ready to serve.

EASY SPINACH CASSEROLE

1 (16 ounce) package frozen chopped spinach
1 (8 ounce) package cream cheese and chives
1 (14 ounce) can fiesta-nacho soup
1 egg, beaten
1½ cups crushed avocado-tortilla chips

✪ Preheat oven to 350°.

✪ Cook spinach according to package directions and drain very well. Blend cream cheese and soup with egg.

✪ Mix with spinach and pour into sprayed baking dish. Top with tortilla chips. Bake for 35 minutes. Serves 8.

CREAMY JALAPENO SPINACH

2 (10 ounce) packages frozen chopped spinach
¼ cup (½ stick) butter, melted
¼ cup chopped onion
3 tablespoons flour
1 cup milk
1 teaspoon seasoned salt
¾ teaspoon celery salt
1 teaspoon white wine Worcestershire sauce
1 (6 ounce) roll jalapeno cheese, cubed
1 cup seasoned breadcrumbs

✪ Preheat oven to 350.

✪ Cook spinach according to package directions and drain well with paper towels.

✪ With butter in skillet, cook onion and flour and stir constantly.

✪ Slowly add milk and cook, stirring constantly, until sauce thickens.

✪ Stir in spinach, ½ teaspoon pepper and all remaining ingredients except breadcrumbs.

✪ Pour into sprayed 2-quart baking dish, sprinkle with breadcrumbs and bake for 20 to 25 minutes. Serves 8.

Zavala County, Texas is the Spinach Capital of the World.

 *Editor's Choice*

★TEXAS FRIED OKRA

1 egg
2 to 3 cups sliced, fresh okra
½ onion, chopped, optional
1 cup cornmeal
½ cup flour
About ½ cup oil for frying

✪ In large shallow bowl, combine egg and 1 tablespoon water and beat with fork just enough to mix well.

✪ Place okra and onion in bowl and mix to thoroughly coat okra with egg mixture.

✪ Place cornmeal, flour, ¾ teaspoon salt and ½ teaspoon pepper in plastic bag. Pour okra-onions in bag and shake vigorously to coat okra well.

✪ Heat oil in large skillet, add breaded okra-onions and fry on medium heat for about 30 minutes, turning every 10 minutes. If skillet dries out, add a little more oil. Serve hot. Serves 6 to 8.

PICKLED OKRA

1 quart young, tender pods, fresh okra
4 cups white vinegar
1 clove garlic
1 jalapeno pepper

✪ Pack okra in sterilized jars.

✪ In saucepan, combine vinegar, 1 cup water, ⅓ cup salt, garlic and pepper and bring to boil. Reduce heat and simmer for about 10 minutes. Pour over okra and seal jars. Store 2 to 3 weeks before serving. Serves 6 to 10.

★GRILLED TEXAS 1015 SUPERSWEET ONIONS

The Texas 1015 SuperSweet Onions are the sweetest onions in the world.

2 large Texas 1015 SuperSweet Onions
10 mild fresh jalapenos
Olive oil

✪ Peel and quarter onions. Slice jalapenos down the center and remove seeds and ribs.

✪ Thread onion and jalapeno alternately on skewers. Brush with olive oil and sprinkle with a little salt and pepper.

✪ Grill until tender with brown grill marks. Serve immediately. Serves 6.

TEXAS 1015 SUPERSWEET ONION ROAST

2 large 1015 SuperSweet Onions or SpringSweet Onions
2 tablespoons butter, divided
Worcestershire sauce

✪ Preheat oven to 350°.

✪ Peel onions and hollow out the center, but do not cut all the way through.

✪ Put 1 tablespoon butter in hollow of each onion, sprinkle a little salt and pepper over each and pour Worcestershire on top and in center.

✪ Bake until onions are tender or microwave on HIGH for about 45 seconds to 1 minute or until onions are tender. Serve immediately. Serves 2.

Editor's Choice

★TEXAS SWEET ONION RINGS

The 1015 SuperSweet or SpringSweet onions were bred to be flatter than regular round onions so that onion rings would be more uniform in size. They were also bred to eliminate tears when you peel and cut them.

2 large Texas 1015 SuperSweet or Spring Sweet onions
2 cups buttermilk
1 cup seasoned breadcrumbs or cracker crumbs
1 cup cornmeal
Canola oil

✪ Slice onions about ¼ inch thick and drop into large bowl. Pour buttermilk over top and marinate about 30 minutes before frying.

✪ In separate bowl mix breadcrumbs, cornmeal, 1 teaspoon salt and ½ teaspoon pepper. Dredge buttermilk-soaked onion rings, a few at a time, through cornmeal mixture. Return to buttermilk to moisten and again dredge through cornmeal mixture.

✪ In deep saucepan or deep fryer with enough oil to cover onion rings, heat oil to 375° to 400° and drop rings into hot oil.

✪ Fry for about 3 minutes or until rings turn golden brown. Remove from fryer with slotted spoon and drain on paper towels. Sprinkle a little salt over top and serve immediately. Serves 6 to 8.

TIP: To make buttermilk, mix 1 cup milk with 1 tablespoon lemon juice or vinegar and let milk rest for about 10 minutes.

CAYENNE-SWEET ONION BAKE

4 to 5 large sweet onions, thinly sliced
1 teaspoon seasoned salt
¼ teaspoon cayenne pepper
1 (16 ounce) package crushed potato chips
1(16 ounce) package shredded Swiss or cheddar cheese, divided
1 (10 ounce) can cream of mushroom soup
¼ cup milk
2 teaspoons white wine Worcestershire sauce

✪ Preheat oven to 350°.

✪ In sprayed 9 x 13-inch baking dish, sprinkle onions with seasoned salt and cayenne pepper and layer with crushed potato chips and half cheese.

✪ In saucepan, combine soup, milk and Worcestershire and heat just enough to mix well. Pour mixture over layers.

✪ Bake for 45 minutes. Before serving, sprinkle remaining cheese over top. Serves 8.

The Big Thicket National Preserve in the piney woods of East Texas is called the American Ark because of the diversity of life in its more than 100,000 acres of swamps, bayous, rivers and creeks preserved by acts of Congress.

HOMESTEAD COLLARD GREENS

2 bunches fresh collard greens
2 (10 ounce) cans chicken broth
5 to 6 strips bacon
1 onion, chopped
1 sweet red bell pepper, chopped
1 tablespoon seasoned salt
1 teaspoon seasoned black pepper
½ teaspoon sugar
1 teaspoon hot sauce, optional

✪ Wash and drain collard greens, cut stems off and coarsely chop greens. Place in large soup kettle and cover with broth and 2 cups water.

✪ Fry bacon in skillet, drain and crumble bacon. In same skillet with bacon drippings, saute onion and bell pepper. Add salt, pepper, sugar and hot sauce, if you like.

✪ Add onion-bell pepper mixture to kettle and heat to full boil. Reduce heat, cover and simmer for 1 hour. Serves 6 to 8.

TRUMPED-UP TURNIPS

5 medium turnips
2 teaspoons sugar
¼ cup (½ stick) butter, melted

✪ Peel and dice turnips. Boil with sugar and 1½ teaspoons salt in enough water to cover until tender and drain. Add butter to turnips and mash. Serve hot. Serves 4 to 6.

SLAP-YOUR-KNEE GOOD POTATOES

6 medium potatoes
½ cup (1 stick) butter, softened
1 tablespoon flour
1 (16 ounce) package shredded cheddar cheese
¾ cup milk

✪ Preheat oven to 350°.

✪ Peel and wash potatoes, slice half potatoes and place in sprayed 3-quart baking dish.

✪ Spread half of butter over potatoes and sprinkle with pepper and flour. Cover with half cheese.

✪ Slice remaining potatoes, place over first layer and add remaining sliced butter.

✪ Pour milk over casserole and sprinkle more pepper. Cover with remaining cheese.

✪ Cover and bake for 1 hour. Serves 8.

TIP: This must be cooked immediately or potatoes will darken. It may be frozen after baking and reheated.

Texas has more farms and more farm acreage than any other state in the U.S. with 181,000 farms and 130,900,000 acres.

HASH BROWN POTATO BAKE

1 (32 ounce) bag frozen hash brown potatoes, thawed
1 onion, chopped
½ cup (1 stick) butter, melted
1 (8 ounce) carton sour cream
1 (10 ounce) can cream of chicken soup
1 (16 ounce) package shredded cheddar cheese
1½ cups crushed corn flakes
2 tablespoons (¼ stick) butter, melted

✪ Preheat oven to 350°.

✪ In large mixing bowl, combine hash brown potatoes, onion, ½ cup (1 stick) melted butter, sour cream, cream of chicken soup and cheese.

✪ Pour in sprayed 9 x 13-inch baking dish. Combine corn flakes and 2 tablespoons (¼ stick) melted butter and sprinkle over casserole. Bake for 50 minutes. Serves 8 to 10.

DINNER-BELL MASHED POTATOES

8 medium to large potatoes
1 (8 ounce) carton sour cream
1 (8 ounce) package cream cheese, softened
½ teaspoon white pepper
Butter

✪ Preheat oven to 325°. Peel, cut up and boil potatoes until tender and drain.

✪ Whip hot potatoes and add sour cream, cream cheese, 1 teaspoon salt and white pepper. Continue whipping until cream cheese melts.

✪ Pour in sprayed 3-quart baking dish. Dot generously with butter. Cover with foil and bake for about 20 minutes. Bake for 10 minutes longer if reheating. Serves 8 to 10.

TIP: This may be made the day before and reheated.

Editor's Choice

UNBELIEVABLE SWEET POTATO CASSEROLE

This is the best sweet potato recipe you will ever make!

1 (29 ounce) can sweet potatoes, drained
⅓ cup evaporated milk
¾ cup sugar
2 eggs, beaten
¼ cup (½ stick) butter, melted
1 teaspoon vanilla

TOPPING:
1 cup packed light brown sugar
⅓ cup butter, melted
½ cup flour
1 cup chopped pecans

✪ Preheat oven to 350°.

✪ Place sweet potatoes in mixing bowl and mash slightly with fork.

✪ Add evaporated milk, sugar, eggs, butter and vanilla and mix well.

✪ Pour into sprayed 7 x 11-inch baking dish.

✪ Mix topping ingredients and sprinkle over casserole.

✪ Bake uncovered for 35 minutes or until crusty on top. Serves 8.

Slim's Tidbit:
*"Eatin' this sweet potato dish is how I got my name, 'Slim'.
I could eat this ever' day just as sure as shootin'."*

Sweet Potato Fritters

1 cup grated sweet potatoes
1 cup sifted flour
2 tablespoons sugar
1 egg, beaten
½ cup milk
Oil for frying

✪ In bowl, combine all ingredients, except oil, with ¼ teaspoon salt. Mix well to form batter.

✪ Drop by tablespoonfuls into kettle of hot oil. When brown, drain, sprinkle with sugar and serve. Serves 4 to 6.

Mexican Rice

3 green onions with tops, chopped
2 cups uncooked rice
½ cup oil
1 small bell pepper, minced
2 tomatoes, seeded, chopped
2 cloves garlic, minced
½ teaspoon cumin
2 (15 ounce) cans chicken broth

✪ Cook onions and rice in oil until onions are translucent and rice is golden color.

✪ Add all remaining ingredients, 1 teaspoon salt and ½ teaspoon pepper. Cook covered 20 to 30 minutes or until rice is tender and absorbs liquid. Serves 6 to 8.

TEXAS RICE

1 onion, chopped
¼ cup (½ stick) butter
4 cups cooked white rice
1 (16 ounce) carton sour cream
1 cup cream-style cottage cheese
¾ teaspoon seasoned salt
1 (4 ounce) can chopped green chilies
1 (16 ounce) package shredded cheddar cheese

✪ Preheat oven to 350°.

✪ In large saucepan, saute onion in butter until translucent, but do not brown.

✪ Remove from heat, and stir in rice, sour cream, cottage cheese, seasoned salt and ¼ teaspoon pepper. Toss lightly to mix well.

✪ Place half rice mixture in sprayed 9 x 13-inch baking dish and sprinkle green chilies over mixture

✪ Sprinkle half cheese on top. Pour remaining rice mixture in casserole and top with remaining cheese.

✪ Bake uncovered for about 35 minutes or until bubbly hot. Serves 8 to 10.

The worst natural disaster in the U.S. took place in 1900 in Galveston when a hurricane generated a 20-foot high tidal wave that completely covered Galveston Island and killed more than 6,000 residents.

GREEN CHILI-CHEESE RICE

1 cup chopped green onions with tops
½ cup chopped bell pepper
¼ cup (½ stick) butter
3 cups cooked white rice
1 (8 ounce) carton sour cream
½ cup cottage cheese
½ teaspoon seasoned salt
¾ teaspoon seasoned pepper
1 (4 ounce) can chopped green chilies
1 (8 ounce) package shredded sharp cheese
Paprika

✪ Preheat oven to 350°.

✪ Saute onion and bell pepper in butter. Remove from heat and combine with ½ teaspoon salt and all remaining ingredients except paprika..

✪ Toss lightly to mix and pour in sprayed casserole dish.

✪ Bake for 30 to 35 minutes. Garnish with paprika. Serves 8.

TIP: One cup chopped ham may be added to make main dish.

SEASONED RED RICE

1 (16 ounce) package smoked sausage, sliced
2 (10 ounce) cans diced tomato and green chilies
3 cups chicken broth
2 teaspoons seasoned salt
1½ cups uncooked long grain rice

✪ Saute sausage in Dutch oven until brown. Stir in tomato and green chilies, broth and seasoning and bring to a boil.

✪ Stir in rice, cover, reduce heat and simmer 25 minutes. Uncover and cook until liquid absorbs. Serves 8 to 10.

The Whole Enchilada!

RUBS, SOPS & MARINADES

BRISKET ★ CHILI

BEEF & TEX-MEX

CHICKEN & TEX-MEX

FISH & CRITTERS

WILD THANGS

Official Mammals of The State of Texas

TEXAS LONGHORN & ARMADILLO

~~ Slim's Tidbit: ~~

"I'd rather watch her walk than eat fried chicken."

TEXAS BARBECUE IS BEEF BRISKET!

In Texas beef brisket is one of the basic food groups. Brisket is synonymous with the word barbecue. In other words, when one says barbecue it means brisket and when one says brisket, it means barbecue. Texans don't barbecue on weekends or use the barbecue to cook on. In Texas barbecue is not a verb and it's not an adjective unless it modifies the word chicken. It is a noun with only one meaning and that meaning is brisket.

Texans grill food or smoke it. You will never hear a native Texan say, "We're going to barbecue this weekend." Grilling doesn't take much time and it's usually done outdoors over a direct fire of charcoal or wood. In fact, grilling was made official in El Paso when they started calling grilled foods al carbon. So you might say El Paso popularized open grilling. Texans grill steaks, marinated beef cuts, hamburgers and chicken, seafood and vegetables.

Texans smoke brisket, ribs, chicken and turkey. Smokin' takes a long time and it's done outdoors in a smoker over indirect heat from a charcoal or wood fire. Barbecue places (commercial restaurants that serve brisket) have huge smokers that are 15 to 20 feet long, about 3 or 4 feet wide and about waist high. All the brisket is laid out on big steel grates that go across the width of the smoker. The grates are black as night and coated with tons of seasonings and brisket juice. A huge metal lid opens with a pulley system so you can see all the fixin's.

The wood of choice for most barbecue places and amateur smokers in Texas is mesquite (ma skeet) wood. Using mesquite wood on smokers is the absolute best use for the wood since it is trash tree, an old scrub, that grows everywhere. It's short, stubby, has killer stickers and is hard to ride around to find cattle. The world recognized the value of mesquite wood when the French started buying it by the truckload to make these real doozy dishes over in Europe.

Other woods used frequently include hickory, pecan and oak. You'll get a different opinion about each of these woods from just about everybody in Texas. The only thing about barbecue that Texans universally agree with is that barbecue is brisket.

Hotter-Than-Blue-Blazes Brisket Rub

4 chipotle peppers, stemmed, seeded, ground
2 ancho chile peppers, stemmed, seeded, ground
½ cup sea salt or coarse salt
3 tablespoons cracked black pepper
3 tablespoons garlic powder
2 tablelspoons paprika
1 tablespoon ground cumin
1 tablespoon dried oregano

✪ In mixing bowl combine all ingredients and whisk together. Store in airtight jar.

✪ Sprinkle on briskets and heavy beef cuts several hours before cooking. Sprinkle on steaks just before grilling.

TIP: **If you are using this rub for chicken, use sparingly and do not marinate as long as beef cuts.**

Brisket Dry Rub

Dry rubs are applied to meat before cooking and allowed to soak into meat. Once the cooking process begins, additional seasoning is usually not added, but brisket sops may be added.

½ cup dried, ground red chile peppers or chili powder
¼ teaspoon paprika
¼ cup freshly ground black pepper
3 tablespoons garlic salt
¼ cup sugar
1 tablespoon dry mustard
1 teaspoon ground oregano

✪   Mix all ingredients in large bowl and store in airtight jar.

✪ Use dry rub seasonings at least 1 hour before cooking. Cover all sides of brisket and pat seasonings into meat.

SMOKE-GETS-IN-YOUR-EYES BRISKET SOP

When you want that smoky flavor, this will get you there.

1 cup (2 sticks) butter
3 cloves garlic, minced
2 jalapenos, stemmed, seeded, minced or 2 teaspoons hot sauce
2 to 3 teaspoons liquid smoke

✪ In small saucepan over low heat, melt butter, cook garlic until clear and stir constantly.

✪ Add all remaining ingredients and cook 2 to 3 minutes. Remove from heat and baste meat with brush.

BEER BRISKET SOP

Just sop this on a brisket when you are grilling or smoking it to keep it moist during the cooking process. Brisket is tender when it is well done.

1 onion, minced
3 cloves garlic, minced
1 (12 ounce) can beer
¼ cup vegetable oil
¼ cup vinegar
2 tablespoons Worcestershire sauce
Chili powder

✪ Put vegetables in large saucepan and pour all remaining ingredients and ½ cup water in saucepan. Add a little salt and pepper and chili powder to taste.

✪ Mix ingredients well and heat on low. Put sop on brisket with pastry brush or rag wrapped around wooden spoon.

✪ Sop brisket 3 to 4 times while cooking.

Pop's Slatherin' Sop

To do a good job slatherin, you need to smear this sop all over the meat. And, you need to do it several times while cooking.

1 (15 ounce) can tomato sauce
1 (18 ounce) bottle steak sauce or barbecue sauce
1 (14 ounce) bottle ketchup
½ cup cooking oil
1 cup (2 sticks) butter
1 to 2 tablespoons hot sauce
1 tablespoon prepared mustard
3 onions, minced
2 cloves garlic, minced
2 to 3 cups packed brown sugar

✪ In saucepan over medium heat, bring tomato sauce, barbecue sauce, ketchup, oil, butter, hot sauce and mustard almost to boil and mix well.

✪ Lower heat, add onions and garlic and stir well.

✪ Slowly pour in brown sugar, stirring constantly, a little at a time. When sugar dissolves, turn heat to simmer and cook covered about 1 to 2 hours. Yield: 6 cups.

———❖———

Basic Barbecue Sauce

1 (15 ounce) can tomato sauce
1 cup vegetable oil
½ cup vinegar
½ cup Worcestershire sauce
1 clove garlic, minced
1 small onion, minced

✪ In large bowl mix all ingredients well with whisk. Refrigerate until ready to use. Yield: 3 cups.

RODEO COWBOY BBQ SAUCE

2 onions, finely minced
1 clove garlic, finely minced
¼ cup (½ stick) butter
1 (14 ounce) bottle ketchup
⅓ cup Worcestershire sauce
2 tablespoons cooking oil
1 to 3 teaspoons chili powder
½ cup packed brown sugar

✪ In saucepan cook onions and garlic in butter until they are translucent.

✪ Add ketchup, 1 cup water, Worcestershire sauce and cooking oil and bring almost to boil, stirring constantly.

✪ Reduce heat, add 2 teaspoons salt and chili powder and mix well.

✪ Slowly add brown sugar while stirring and simmer for about 20 to 30 minutes. Yield: 4 cups.

The National Cowgirl Hall of Fame in Fort Worth is the only museum in the world commemorating notable western women and their pioneering spirit.

The largest horse-drawn parade in the world is the All-Western Parade that kicks off the Southwestern Exposition and Livestock Show and Rodeo in Fort Worth.

Editor's Choice

HOMER'S BEST MARINADE

Use this marinade on any beef you plan to grill or smoke. It is really good and that's the gospel truth.

1 cup red wine
2 teaspoons Worcestershire sauce
2 teaspoons garlic powder
1 cup oil
¼ cup ketchup
2 teaspoons sugar
2 tablespoons vinegar
1 teaspoon marjoram
1 teaspoon rosemary
½ teaspoon seasoned pepper

✪ Mix all ingredients for marinade with 1 teaspoon salt and stir well.

✪ Marinate beef several hours before cooking. Yield: 2½ cups.

BARBECUE MARINADE

4 to 5 lemons
1 teaspoon sea salt
1 teaspoon cracked black pepper
1 tablespoon ground, dried red chile flakes
4 cloves garlic, minced
½ cup cilantro, minced
¼ cup fresh oregano
¼ cup fresh basil
¼ cup fresh chives
½ cup extra virgin olive oil

✪ Juice lemons to equal ⅓ cup and pour in mixing bowl. Add sea salt and whisk until salt dissolves.

✪ Add all remaining ingredients and whisk thoroughly. Use immediately and marinate several hours for beef and less time for chicken. Yield: 1½ cups.

★ TEXAS BEEF BRISKET

1 (4 to 5 pound) beef brisket, trimmed
2 tablespoons garlic powder
2 tablespoons black pepper
2 tablespoons seasoned salt
¼ cup liquid smoke
3 tablespoons Worcestershire sauce

✪ Prepare foil to seal brisket inside with marinade.

✪ Place brisket inside foil and make sure marinade will not leak.

✪ Season brisket with garlic powder, black pepper and seasoned salt and pour in liquid smoke and Worcestershire sauce.

✪ Seal foil tightly, place on baking pan and refrigerate overnight.

✪ Place baking pan and brisket in oven and bake at 300° for 4 hours or until meat is very tender. Serves 6 to 8.

―――◈―――

Slim's Tidbit:

"Texans have a long history of raisin' beef and bein raised on beef. Babies learn how to chew eatin' brisket. They drink cream gravy out of a Tommy-Tippy cup and cut their teeth on Texas Spareribs. Beef is a way of life, a way of thinkin' and a way of livin'. If you ever want to know, "Where's the beef?", well, it's right here in Texas, sure as shootin'."

★SMOKED BRISKET

You'll get as many different opinions about smoking briskets as you will about barbecue sops, marinades and cooking methods. This just happens to be one that's simple, but very good.

1 (4 to 5 pound) beef brisket
Seasoned salt
Cracked black pepper

✪ Season brisket at room temperature about 1 hour before cooking.

✪ Soak mesquite or hickory chips in water or beer at least 1 hour.

✪ Prepare mesquite or hickory wood fire or charcoal fire in fire box at 1 end of smoker. When fire burns down, add small pieces of mesquite or hickory to fire.

✪ Put brisket on rack away from fire, close lid and begin smoking process.

✪ Add wood chips several times to make sure enough smoke is circulating. Smoke for about 3 to 4 hours.

✪ Remove brisket from smoker and cook in covered, roasting pan with about 1 cup water at 300° for about 2 to 3 hours or until fork tender. Check water to make sure pan and brisket do not dry.

✪ Remove from oven and cool about 1 hour before slicing. Slice across the grain in thin pieces. Serves 6 to 8.

It is standard in barbecue cafes in Texas for brisket to be served with onion slices, pickle slices and a toothpick. Some places also serve corn-on-the-cob, potato salad and pinto beans.

REAL SIMPLE BRISKET

1 (4 to 6 pound) trimmed beef brisket
Seasoned salt
Seasoned pepper
1 (1 ounce) package onion soup mix
¼ cup Worcestershire sauce

✪ Preheat oven to 375°.

✪ Place brisket in roaster or Dutch oven. Generously sprinkle brisket with seasoned salt and seasoned pepper. Spread onion soup mix over top of brisket.

✪ Pour Worcestershire sauce in and add about 1 cup water. Cook for 1 hour.

✪ Reduce heat to 300° and cook 3 to 4 hours or until brisket is tender. Serves 8 to 10.

TIP: Brisket should be well done and fork-tender.

Slim's Tidbit:
"Ya have ta cook brisket for a long time
or it's gonna be tougher 'an a boot."

R eal Texas barbecue is brisket cooked slowly from the indirect heat and smoke of a wood fire not directly under the meat with heat kept at a very low temperature.

Fancy Beef Brisket

1 (5 to 6 pound) beef brisket
1 (4-ounce) bottle liquid smoke
1 teaspoon celery salt
1 teaspoon paprika
¼ teaspoon ground nutmeg
1 teaspoon garlic powder
1 teaspoon onion salt
1 teaspoon seasoned pepper
1 tablespoon brown sugar

✪ Cover brisket with liquid smoke, cover with foil and refrigerate overnight.

✪ Combine celery salt, paprika, nutmeg, garlic powder, onion salt, pepper and brown sugar.

✪ Sprinkle brisket with mixture and cover tightly with foil.

✪ Bake for 2 hours at 325°.

✪ Loosen foil and bake for 5 hours more at 200°.

✪ Remove meat from pan and set aside at least 1 hour before slicing. Strain any grease from pan juices. Slice brisket very thin across the grain and serve with hot degreased liquid. Serves 8 to 10.

Wood fires such as hickory, oak and pecan smoke better than charcoal fires and are used for real Texas barbecue. Mesquite is also used, but burns hotter and faster.

The Houston Livestock Show and Rodeo World Championship BBQ Cook-Off is held in late January and is one of the biggest in the state.

BRISKET WITH BARBECUE SAUCE

1 (4 to 5 pound) trimmed brisket
2 tablespoons Worcestershire sauce
Seasoned salt
Garlic powder

BARBECUE SAUCE:
1 cup ketchup
⅓ cup Worcestershire sauce
¾ cup packed brown sugar
1 tablespoon lemon juice

✪ Preheat oven to 425°.

✪ Place brisket in shallow baking pan and pour Worcestershire over brisket.

✪ Sprinkle with seasoned salt, garlic powder and pepper and add ¼ cup water to pan. Cover with foil. Bake for 30 minutes.

✪ Lower oven to 250° and cook for about 3 to 4 hours.

✪ While brisket is cooking, mix all sauce ingredients in saucepan.

✪ When brisket is done, add pan dripping to saucepan. Refrigerate brisket so it will cut nicely.

✪ Slice brisket in thin slices, warm sauce in saucepan and pour sauce over slices. Return to oven to warm brisket. Serves 8.

TIP: Use ketchup-based barbecue sauces only in the last 30 to 45 minutes of cooking or when warming brisket so sauce does not burn.

DOWNTOWN BRISKET

1 (5 to 7 pound) trimmed beef brisket
1 (4 ounce) bottle liquid smoke
1 teaspoon garlic salt
1 teaspoon onion salt
1 teaspoon celery salt
1 teaspoon seasoned pepper

BARBECUE SAUCE:
1 (16 ounce) bottle ketchup
½ cup packed brown sugar
1 teaspoon prepared mustard
1½ teaspoons garlic powder
2 tablespoons Worcestershire sauce
⅛ teaspoon cayenne pepper
¼ cup vinegar

✪ Place brisket in large baking pan and coat generously with liquid smoke. Sprinkle spices over brisket, cover pan with foil and refrigerate overnight.

✪ Pour off about three-fourths of liquid smoke. Combine all barbecue sauce ingredients and pour over brisket.

✪ Cook at 350° for 1 hour. Lower heat to 255° and cook for about 5 more hours.

✪ Cool brisket at least 1 hour before slicing.

✪ Pour sauce from baking pan into saucepan and boil about 15 minutes until it thickens enough to serve over brisket. Serves 10 to 12.

SLOW-COOKER CORNED BEEF BRISKET

This is a beef brisket cured in a salt water or brine solution.

4 ribs celery, chopped
3 medium onions, quartered
1 (2 to3 pound) corned beef brisket, trimmed
2 tablespoons whole black peppercorns
2 bay leaves
1 large head green cabbage
8 to 10 small red or new potatoes, quartered
10 to 12 small carrots
2 tablespoons butter, melted

❂ Place celery and onions in 5-quart slow cooker and place brisket on top. Sprinkle peppercorns and bay leaves on top of brisket and add 3 to 4 cups water.

❂ Cook on LOW for 8 to 9 hours or until brisket is fork tender.

❂ Place brisket on platter and discard liquid. Allow about 10 to 20 minutes before slicing.

❂ Place cabbage, potatoes, carrots and ¼ cup water in large microwave-safe bowl. Microwave on HIGH for about 7 minutes. Stir and rotate in microwave.

❂ Microwave again on HIGH for about 5 minutes or until vegetables are tender.

❂ Pour butter over vegetables, season with salt and pepper and arrange around corned beef on platter. Serve immediately. Serves 6 to 8.

CHILI – THE OFFICIAL STATE DISH OF TEXAS

At one time chili was just another bowl of stew until a Dallas newspaperman, Frank X. Tolbert, challenged Wick Fowler, another newspaperman, and H. Allen Smith, a humorist, to a chili cook-off. They began the first World Championship Chili Cook-Off held in the ghost town of Terlingua, Texas in the Big Bend country. The contest has three criteria: taste, appearance and aroma. And let the message go out far and wide, any meat may be used (and probably has), but NO beans, pasta, rice and other similar items are allowed.

The Cook-Off today has grown to immense proportions in size and eccentric behaviors. Entrants must now qualify to enter by a point system and the competition has expanded to include the Chili Showmanship Competition featuring theme and originality, costumes, booth set-up, action and audience appeal. To summarize the event let it be known that anything goes. . . except beans. Beans are definitely banned and left somewhere outside the unmarked city limits of Terlingua.

Today, chili cook-offs are held all over the world, but the most famous chili cook-off was and still is the World Championship Chili Cook-Off in Terlingua, Texas. Well, I'll be.

⟶ Slim's Tidbit: ⟵

"A Word of Warning: If you're enterin' an official Texas Chili Cook-Off, you'll be disqualified if there're beans in your chili. As a past winner and judge of Chili Cook-Offs, I don't hesitate to disqualify many a bowl of chili 'cause a beans, even 'mid tha moans and groans of outraged Northerners. In fact, I rather enjoyed their ignorance. Another little tidbit you might need some day is that a bowl of chili should be a dark red color. That's why it's called a 'Bowl of Red'. Git it?"

★A BOWL OF RED
Proper name for Real Texas Chili, make no beans about it

½ cup beef suet or vegetable oil
3 pounds sirloin steak, cubed
6 to 8 dried chile colorado peppers, ground or 4 to 5 dried chipotle
    chile peppers, ground
1 to 2 whole jalapeno peppers, divided
4 to 6 cloves garlic, minced
½ cup paprika
2 tablespoons ground cumin
1 tablespoon oregano
2 tablespoons masa harina, optional

✪ Cook suet until fat separates from connective tissue or vegetable oil for
   healthier cooking. Remove suet and brown sirloin on all sides.

✪ Pour sirloin and oil from skillet in large kettle or roasting pan. Add
   ground chile peppers, 1 whole jalapeno and enough water to be about
   2 inches above meat.

✪ Bring water to boil, reduce heat and simmer about 2 to 3 hours. Stir
   occasionally and skim off grease.

✪ Add garlic, paprika, cumin, oregano and 2 teaspoons salt, cover and
   simmer another 1 hour. Stir occasionally and skim off grease.

✪ Check seasonings and add whole jalapeno if not hot enough. Add
   masa harina if chili is too thin and simmer another 30 minutes to 1
   hour. Serves 8 to 10.

TIP: Masa harina is flour made from masa, sun-dried or oven-dried corn
      kernels used to make corn tortillas. It's used as a thickening agent in
      this recipe.

★CHAMPIONSHIP CHILI

Real chili is worth the effort! Boy I mean!

Oil
3 to 3½ pounds stew meat
1 onion, chopped
1 (15 ounce) can tomato sauce
10 to 12 tablespoons dried chile colorado peppers, ground, seeded
1 to 2 tablespoons ground cumin
1 tablespoon oregano
1 to 2 jalapenos

✪ In a little oil, brown stew meat and onion in large kettle or roasting pan.

✪ Add tomato sauce, ground chilies, cumin, oregano, 2 teaspoons salt and enough water to be 2 inches above meat and bring to a boil. Reduce heat and simmer for about 2 hours. Stir occasionally.

✪ Taste for seasonings and add whole jalapeno if more "hot" is needed. Simmer another 1 hour.

✪ Serve immediately with crackers or wait until the next day to serve. Some people believe real chili needs time for flavors to blend. Serves 8 to 10.

TIP: Chiles colorado are New Mexican Reds and are about 5 to7 inches long, about 1 to 2 inches wide, dark-red brown and slightly hot. If you have never ground dried chilies, use food processor, blender or coffee grinder. They will live through it and so will you. These are great peppers to use because you do not have to peel them when they are dry.

There are many who claim chili as their invention, but only Texans can truthfully, historically and by necessity lay claim to originating chili. Immigrants from the Canary Islands may have brought the knowledge of spices, but by the time they figured out chili, they were Texans.

BIG-TIME CHILI

You know the chili's good when it makes your nose run.

2 onions, chopped
¼ cup oil
5 pounds ground beef
1 (15 ounce) can diced tomatoes
1 (6 ounce) can tomato paste
¼ teaspoon cayenne pepper
4 to 6 tablespoons chili powder
2 teaspoons ground cumin
1 tablespoon paprika

✪ In roasting pan or kettle, saute onions in oil and brown ground beef.

✪ Mix in all remaining ingredients and 2 teaspoons salt and bring to boil. Reduce heat and simmer for 3 hours.

✪ Stir several times and add water if needed. Serves 10 to 12.

Slim's Tidbit:

"Now, ground beef is ok in chili, but most Texans who respect tha 'ficial State Dish of tha Great State of Texas 'll put steak in their chili. And, if you think somethin' else 'sides beef goes in chili, you gotta another think comin'."

The basic ingredients of chili include beef suet or flavored liquid, beef steak or roast, chilies, cumin, garlic and oregano. Many people stray from the basics to create some exotic dish that is not even close to chili. To be true to real chili remember the basics and make a meat dish, not a stew or soup.

★ORIGINAL CHILI CON CARNE

"Chili con carne" means chili with meat and is the same thing as "Chili" or in Texas it is a "Bowl of Red".

2 to 3 pounds cubed sirloin or tenderloin
½ cup (1 stick) butter
1 (15 ounce) can tomato sauce or 1 (15 ounce) can diced tomatoes
  with liquid
2 onions, chopped
4 to 6 cloves garlic, minced
¼ cup chili powder
1 tablespoon ground cumin
2 teaspoons oregano

✪ Brown sirloin in butter in large skillet. Reduce heat to low and add 1 teaspoon salt and all remaining ingredients.

✪ Simmer covered for about 2 to 3 hours. Stir occasionally and add ½ to 1 cup water if necessary.

✪ Remove cover, taste for flavor and adjust seasonings if needed. Serves 6 to 8.

Chili booths were common in San Antonio during the late 19th century on the city's plazas. Here bowls of *chile con carne* were served by *senoritas* to the many customers who gathered around. The earliest description of San Antonio's *chile con carne* appeared in 1828, when J.C. Clopper observed that Mexican families frequently had to make do with a small amount of meat which… 'is generally cut into a kind of hash with nearly as many peppers as there are pieces of meat–this is all stewed together.' By 1893 the dish was so popular that there was a San Antonio Chili Stand at the Chicago World's Fair. Shortly after the opening of the 20th century the popular chili stands were forced out of business by strict health regulations and restrictions. With them passed a colorful bit of San Antonio history."

The Melting Pot: Ethnic Cuisine in Texas
The Institute of Texan Cultures of The University of Texas at San Antonio

EASY CHILI

2 pounds lean groundchuck
1 onion, chopped
1 (1¾ ounce packages chili seasoning mix
1 (46 ounce) can tomato juice

✪ Cook beef and onion in Dutch oven, stir until meat crumbles, browns and drain.

✪ Stir in remaining ingredients.

✪ Bring mixture to boil, reduce heat and simmer. Stir occasionally for about 2 hours. Serves 6 to 8.

EASY CHILI CASSEROLE

1 (40 ounce) can chili
1 (4 ounce) can chopped green chilies
1 (2¼ ounce) can sliced ripe olives, drained
1 (8 ounce) package shredded cheddar cheese
2 cups ranch-flavored tortilla chips, crushed

✪ Preheat oven to 350°.

✪ In bowl, combine all ingredients. Transfer to sprayed 3-quart baking dish.

✪ Bake, uncovered, for about 35 minutes or until bubbly. Serves 5 to 6.

CHICKEN-FRIED IS A WAY OF COOKIN'

Chicken-fried is a way of cooking in Texas and a general all-purpose word meaning anything pan-fried. Corn-fed beef just isn't "dressed" until it steps out of a cast-iron skillet wearing a golden brown coat.

Texans have been serving up larrupin' good, chicken-fried entrees since the days beef suet and chicken fat were the only buddies to the cast-iron skillet. Choice cuts of beef don't need any decoration, but the less tender cuts of beef may require blunt-force trauma to tender-'em-up some and a little cream gravy to make 'em fit for a king.

Chicken-fried batter can even enhance nearly all the farmer's market produce, like okra, yellow squash, zucchini, asparagus and tomatoes, out of the north-forty garden. It can even doctor-up some catfish from a rancher's stock tank, frog legs from the cat-tails and just about anything else you want to throw in the skillet.

Fork-tender meat nestled in a delicate, crispy crust will make a Texan purr like a boardinghouse cat. Boy, I mean!

CLASSIC CREAM GRAVY

The Texas trilogy, pan drippins, milk and flour, team up to give entrees the perfect sidekick, cream gravy. Texans will douse, dunk it and when it's too thin to "tighten up", drink it.

Cream gravy is the forgivin' guest at every Texas table. It can doctor up just about any cut of beef, even those hammered out of their minds to make 'em tender. If the gravy's so thick that it takes three cousins and a half-dead, step-neighbor to lift it out of the skillet, milk can be added to thin it 'til it's just right. You can't beat the flavor when pan drippings, milk and a little flour come together.

Be on the lookout for a desperate Texan wearing sunglasses in a grocery store. He'll probably be slippin' a package of peppered gravy mix in his grocery basket on the sly. You'll know he's probably all hat and no cattle.

 *Editor's Choice*

★CLASSIC CREAM GRAVY

A lot of Texans think this is a main course.

Bacon drippings
3 tablespoons flour
1½ cups milk

❂ The best cream gravy is made in the same skillet used to fry chicken, steak, pork sausage or bacon. The "pan drippings" add their own special seasonings.

❂ If you do not have pan "drippings", pour a little bacon grease in skillet, heat and add flour and ½ teaspoon each of salt and pepper. Stir to mix well.

❂ Turn heat to high and slowly pour milk into skillet while stirring constantly until gravy thickens.

❂ When gravy reaches right consistency, pour into bowl and serve with biscuits, meat or drink it straight from bowl. Serves 4.

※※※

Slim's Tidbit:

"In Texas chili is chili or it's a pepper. 'Chile' is just some French word from New Mexico. There ain't any chiles in Texas, but we got a lot a peppers. You don't have to say chile peppers, you just say peppers or just say jalapenos (hal a pain yos)."

Editor's Choice

★LONE STAR CHICKEN-FRIED STEAK AND CREAM GRAVY

This is a true Texas original! Cowboys ate these steaks on trail drives and cowboys and Texans today continue the tradition. Chicken-fried steak is just part of Texas.

2 pounds round steak, tenderized
1 ¼ cups flour
Seasoned pepper
2 eggs, slightly beaten
½ cup milk
Oil

Cream gravy:
6 to 8 tablespoons pan drippings
6 tablespoons flour
3 cups milk

○ Trim tenderized steak and cut into 6 to 8 pieces. Combine flour, 1 teaspoon salt and pepper. Dredge all steak pieces in flour mixture until lightly coated.

○ Combine eggs and milk. Dip steak into egg mixture, dredge again in flour and get plenty of flour pressed into steak.

○ Heat about ½ inch oil in heavy skillet and fry steak pieces until golden brown.

○ To make gravy, move steaks to warm oven. Add flour to drippings in skillet, stir constantly and cook until flour begins to brown.

○ Add milk slowly and stir until gravy thickens. Season with ½ teaspoon salt and ¼ teaspoon pepper and serve in bowl or over steaks and mashed potatoes. Serves 4 to 6.

COWPOKE STEAK AND GRAVY

1 to 1½ pounds tenderized round steak
Oil
1 (1 ounce) envelope onion soup mix
1 (10 ounce) can golden mushroom soup

✪ Preheat oven to 325°.

✪ Cut round steak into serving-size pieces and season with salt and pepper.

✪ Lightly brown steak pieces in small amount of oil. Transfer steak to large baking pan. Sprinkle onion soup mix over steak.

✪ In saucepan, combine soup and ¾ cup water and heat just enough to mix well. Pour over steak pieces.

✪ Cover and bake for 1 hour and check to see if more water is needed. Continue to bake for another 30 minutes. Serves 4 to 5.

Texas produces more cattle with 14.8 million head than any other state in the U.S.

Texas produces more sheep with 1.7 million head than any other state in the U.S.

★TEXAS CALF FRIES

A real delicacy around the Fort Worth Stockyards and Texas ranches

3 to 4 pounds calf fries
1 to 2 cans beer
2 to 3 eggs, beaten
2 cups cornmeal

✪ Drop calf fries into very hot water, but not boiling, and leave for 3 to 4 minutes. Remove from water, peel membrane and dry with paper towel.

✪ Quarter calf fries and season well with salt and pepper.

✪ In large bowl pour 1 can beer and place all calf fries into bowl. Add more beer if needed to cover calf fries. Soak calf fries for about 30 minutes to 1 hour.

✪ Remove calf fries from beer and dip in beaten eggs. Roll in cornmeal and pat cornmeal into fries.

✪ In large skillet with hot oil, place calf fries in skillet and brown on all sides. Drain and serve. Serves 6 to 8.

TIP: **Pan-frying is a Texas way of cooking and when it is done correctly it is not as bad for you as one might think. When fried at 350°, the outside of the meat is seared to seal in the meat's juices without soaking up oil.**

Editor's Choice

HOMER'S DYNAMITE MARINATED BEEF KEBABS

You will not believe how good this is and how impressive it looks. It is a real treat!

2 to 2½ pounds sirloin steak
Fresh mushrooms
Green, red and yellow bell peppers
Small onions
Cherry tomatoes

MARINADE:
1 cup red wine
2 teaspoons Worcestershire sauce
2 teaspoons garlic powder
1 cup oil
¼ cup ketchup
2 teaspoons sugar
2 tablespoons vinegar
1 teaspoon marjoram
1 teaspoon rosemary
½ teaspoon seasoned pepper

✪ Cut meat into 1½ to 2-inch pieces and quarter bell peppers.

✪ Mix all ingredients and 1 teaspoon salt for marinade and stir well.

✪ Marinate steak pieces 3 to 4 hours.

✪ Alternate meat, mushrooms, peppers, onions and cherry tomatoes on skewers.

✪ Cook on charcoal grill, turn on all sides and baste frequently with remaining marinade. Serves 8.

Editor's Choice

PREACHER POT ROAST AND GRAVY

When the preacher comes for dinner after church on Sunday, this is a regular dish.

4 to 5 round boneless rump roast
Seasoned salt
Seasoned pepper
Garlic powder
6 medium potatoes, peeled, quartered
8 carrots, peeled, quartered
3 onions, peeled, quartered

GRAVY:
3 tablespoons cornstarch

❂ Preheat oven to 350°.

❂ Set roast in roasting pan and sprinkle liberally with seasoned salt, seasoned pepper and garlic powder. Add 1 cup water.

❂ Roast for about 3 hours or until it is fork-tender.

❂ Add potatoes, carrots and onions. Cook another 35 to 40 minutes or until vegetables are tender.

❂ Place roast on platter and arrange potatoes, carrots and onion around it.

❂ To make gravy, combine cornstarch and ¾ cup water and add to juices left in roasting pan.

❂ Add ½ teaspoon salt and cook on high on stove until gravy thickens, stirring constantly. Serve with roast. Serves 8.

BEEF-STUFFED CABBAGE

1 pound lean ground beef
¾ pound ground pork
1 cup cooked rice
1 small onion, minced
2 eggs, beaten
1 teaspoon caraway seeds
1 teaspoon prepared minced garlic
1 teaspoon seasoned salt
½ to 1 cup prepared seasoned breadcrumbs
1 large head cabbage
2 (15 ounce) cans stewed tomatoes
2 tablespoons cornstarch, optional

✪ Preheat oven to 350°.

✪ In bowl, combine beef, pork, rice, onion, eggs, caraway seeds, garlic, seasoned salt, 1 teaspoon pepper and breadcrumbs. Use only enough breadcrumbs to keep meat mixture together, then mix well.

✪ Place cabbage in large saucepan of boiling water and let rest for 5 minutes. Remove cabbage, cool and peel off about 12 outer leaves. (You may need to cut largest leaves in half.) Trim thickest part of stem from leaves.

✪ Shred about 1 cup remaining cabbage and place in bottom of sprayed 10 x 15-inch baking dish .

✪ Divide beef-pork mixture into 12 portions, pat into roll and wrap each portion in cabbage leaf. Fasten with toothpicks if necessary.

✪ Place each roll over shredded cabbage. Mix cornstarch with stewed tomatoes until it dissolves and pour over cabbage rolls. Bake covered for 55 minutes. Serves 8 to 10.

SAVORY MEAT LOAF

1½ pounds lean ground beef
2 eggs
2 tablespoons dried minced onion
1 teaspoon seasoned salt
1 teaspoon minced garlic
¾ cup prepared seasoned breadcrumbs
2 tablespoons Worcestershire sauce
1 (8 ounce) can tomato sauce

✪ Preheat oven to 350°. In large bowl, combine ground beef, eggs, minced onion, seasoned salt, ½ teaspoon pepper, garlic, breadcrumbs, Worcestershire and tomato sauce.

✪ Shape into loaf and place in shallow baking pan. Bake uncovered for 45 to 50 minutes. Serves 4 to 6.

BLACK-EYED PEA FIESTA SUPPER

1½ pounds lean ground beef
1 onion, chopped
1 teaspoon minced garlic
1 tablespoon oil
2 (15 ounce) cans black-eyed peas, drained
1 (10 ounce) can chopped tomatoes and green chilies
2 (10 ounce) cans fiesta nacho cheese soup
8 to 10 corn tortillas, cut in eighths
1 (8 ounce) package shredded Mexican 4-cheese blend cheese

✪ Preheat oven to 350°. In large skillet, brown beef, onion and garlic in oil and drain. Add peas, tomatoes, green chilies and soups and mix well. In sprayed 9 x 13-inch baking dish, layer beef-vegetable mixture and tortillas twice.

✪ Top with half cheese and bake for 30 minutes. Remove from oven, sprinkle remaining cheese over top and return to oven just until cheese melts. Serves 4 to 6.

 *Editor's Choice*

★TEXAS CORNY DOGS

Here's a great recipe for homemade corny dogs.

1 cup flour
1 cup yellow cornmeal
¼ cup sugar
4 teaspoons baking powder
2 eggs
½ cup milk
¼ cup oil
1 (10 count) beef wieners
10 ice cream sticks
Oil

✪ Mix flour, cornmeal, sugar, baking powder ¾ teaspoon salt, eggs, milk and ¼ cup oil in deep bowl and blend well.

✪ Put each wiener on ice cream stick. Dip into batter; then drop into deep fryer and cook until golden brown. Remove from fryer and drain. Serves 4 to 5.

The first corny dog was made by Neil Fletcher in his kitchen in the 1940's. The corny dog was served at the State Fair of Texas and it became a popular mealtime treat nationwide.

BEEF JERKY

Making beef jerky is a little like making barbecue sauce because you really doctor up the recipe every time you make it. This is a good basic one and you can take it from here.

½ cup **Worcestershire sauce**
1 cup **soy sauce**
6 to 8 **cloves garlic, minced**
4 to 5 **tablespoons lemon pepper**
4 to 5 **pounds flank steak**

✪ Pour Worcestershire, soy sauce and garlic in large glass baking dish and put flank steak in it. Marinate meat for 2 to 3 hours.

✪ Remove steak from dish and put on cutting board. Season meat liberally with lemon pepper and lightly with salt. Press seasonings into meat.

✪ Slice steak with grain in long, thin strips about 5 x 1 x ¼ inch. Move meat around so that seasonings get on all sides.

✪ Marinate for a while or place strips of meat on baking sheets right away, but do not overlap strips.

✪ Cook in oven at 175° for about 6 to 8 hours. Leave the oven door slightly open to circulate air. Yield: About 2 quarts.

OPTIONAL BEEF JERKY INGREDIENTS:

Freshly ground black pepper
Ground chiles Colorado (dried New Mexico Reds)
Ground chipotle chiles
Seasoned pepper
Garlic pepper
Chili powder
Dried onion flakes
Teriyaki sauce
Hot sauce

TEXAS FAJITAS
(Fah-HEE-tas) One of the basic food groups in Texas

Fajitas are original to Texas and probably have their roots in the Texas cattle drives. Traditionally, fajitas are strips of skirt steak, marinated, grilled and cut in strips about 4 inches long and ½ inch wide. These are served with flour tortillas and a variety of vegetables. Fajitas are amazing not only for their flavor, but also because such an inexpensive cut of beef is so delicious. Fajitas are known and served all over the world.

★TEXAS BEEF FAJITAS

MARINADE:
1 cup prepared salsa or fresh salsa (page 15)
1 cup bottled Italian dressing
2 tablespoons lemon juice
2 tablespoons chopped green onions
1 teaspoon garlic powder
1 teaspoon celery salt

2 pounds skirt steak
Flour tortillas

FILLING FOR FAJITAS:
Prepared salsa or fresh salsa (page 15)
Guacamole (page 35)
Grilled onions
Grilled bell peppers
Chopped tomatoes
Shredded cheese
Sour cream

✪ Mix all marinade ingredients and 1 teaspoon pepper in large bowl.

✪ Slice skirt steak into ½ inch wide strips and marinate for several hours.

✪ Grill or pan-fry skirt steak and put on tortillas with selected accompaniments. Serves 6 to 8.

★QUICK AND EASY FAJITAS

You don't have to get fancy or complicated with fajitas. Just the basics work very nicely.

1 to 2 pounds skirt or flank steak
4 limes
1 tablespoon minced, fresh garlic or 1 teaspoon garlic powder
Oil

✪ Trim fat from steak and place in bowl.

✪ Mix limes, garlic and 1 teaspoon pepper and pour over steak. Marinate about 6 to 8 hours.

✪ Remove steak and discard marinade. Slice steak in thin slices about 4 inches long and ½ inch wide. Cook in heavy skillet with a little oil.

✪ Serve with flour tortillas. Serves 6 to 8.

―――――>◦◇◦<―――――

⤛⤜ Slim's Tidbit: ⤛⤜

"Have ya ever noticed how Murka (Lyndon Johnson's America) gits hold a somethin' good and just forgets who hatched it. Well, Texans hatched these faheeta thangs, but not 'cause they wanted some ol' tough piece a meat. Texans have a histry a makin' do with what they got no matter how pore it is. Reminds me a when we 'as so pore, Sunday supper was fried water. Now, Texans make something good out of something cheap like skirt steak and now faheetas cost as much as a regler steak and they're on ever' menu in tha country, not just Meskun food places. Well, just cut off my legs and call me Shorty!"

★BEEF BURRITOS

A flour tortilla and some refried beans make this a nice little sandwich Texas-style.

1 pound ground beef
1 tablespoon chili powder
2 onions, chopped
4 to 6 flour tortillas, warmed
1 (15 ounce) can refried beans
1 (8 ounce) package shredded Mexican 4-cheese blend
1 tomato, chopped
Salsa

✪ In heavy skillet brown ground beef with 1 teaspoon salt and chili powder.

✪ Drain grease, add onions and cook until onions are translucent.

✪ In saucepan, heat refried beans. Spread several tablespoons refried beans on warmed, flour tortilla.

✪ Add ground beef, cheese and tomato and roll up like an envelope, folding up 2 ends and rolling. Serve with salsa. Serves 4 to 6.

⟹◆⟸

The oldest family-owned Mexican restaurant chain in the U.S. is El Fenix. Mike Martinez Sr. started his restaurant in 1918 in Dallas and changed its name to El Fenix in 1922 when he began serving all Mexican dishes. He was responsible for developing the combination plates now seen in all Mexican restaurants nationwide.

★SOFT BEEF TACOS

2 pounds lean ground beef
2 tablespoons chili powder
1 (14 ounce) can kidney beans
1 large onion, chopped, divided
14 to 16 corn tortillas
3 large tomatoes, chopped
1 tablespoon minced cilantro
1 (12 ounce) package shredded cheddar cheese, divided

✪ Preheat oven to 350°.

✪ Brown ground beef, add chili powder and 1 tablespoon salt and cook for about 5 minutes.

✪ Put several tablespoons of meat, several tablespoons of beans and 1 teaspoon onion in middle of each tortilla, roll up and place side by side in sprayed 10 x 15-inch baking dish.

✪ Combine tomatoes, remaining onion, and cilantro and sprinkle evenly over rolled tortillas.

✪ Spread cheese over top of tomatoes and bake for 10 to 15 minutes or until cheese melts.

✪ Serve hot with chips. Serves 6 to 8.

The first commercially packaged chili powder and canned chilies were produced by William Gebhardt of New Braunfels. In 1896 Gebhardt opened a factory in San Antonio to supply the demand.

TACO PIE

1 pound lean ground beef
1 green bell pepper, chopped
2 jalapeno peppers, seeded, chopped
Oil
1 (15 ounce) can Mexican stewed tomatoes
1 tablespoon chili powder
½ teaspoon minced garlic
1 (8 ounce) package shredded sharp cheddar cheese
1 (6 ounce) package corn muffin mix
1 egg
⅔ cup milk

✪ Preheat oven to 375°.

✪ In large skillet, brown ground beef, bell pepper and jalapeno peppers in oil and drain. Add ½ teaspoon salt, tomatoes, 1 cup water, chili powder and garlic. Cook on medium heat for about 10 to15 minutes or until most of liquid cooks out, but not dry.

✪ Pour into sprayed 9 x 13-inch glass baking dish. Sprinkle cheese on top.

✪ Combine corn muffin mix, egg and milk and beat well. Pour over top of cheese.

✪ Bake for 25 minutes or until corn muffin mix is light brown.

✪ Remove from oven and allow to set about 10 minutes before serving. Serves 4 to 6.

TIP: This may be made ahead of time. Mix all ingredients except corn muffin mix and mix corn muffin mix just before cooking.

★TRADITIONAL BEEF ENCHILADAS

1½ pounds lean ground beef
1 onion, finely chopped
1 (8 ounce) can tomato sauce
1 teaspoon minced garlic
1 teaspoon chili powder
½ teaspoon ground cumin
10 corn tortillas
Oil
1 (12 ounce) package shredded cheddar cheese
2 (10 ounce) cans enchilada sauce

✪ Preheat oven to 350°.

✪ In skillet, brown beef and onion together and drain. Add tomato sauce, garlic, chili powder, cumin and 1 teaspoon salt and heat mixture thoroughly.

✪ With oil in large skillet, soften each tortilla and place on wax paper. Spoon about 3 heaping tablespoons of beef-onion mixture and 2 tablespoons cheese on each tortilla.

✪ Roll up and place each tortilla seam side down in sprayed 9 x 13-inch baking dish.

✪ Add any remaining beef-onion mixture to enchilada sauce and pour over enchiladas in baking dish.

✪ Sprinkle remaining shredded cheese and bake for 20 to 25 minutes. Serves 6 to 8.

BEEF-ENCHILADA CASSEROLE

1½ pounds ground beef
1 (1 ounce) package taco seasoning mix
Oil
8 flour or corn tortillas
1 (8 ounce) package shredded cheddar cheese, divided
1 (10 ounce) can enchilada sauce
1 (4 ounce) can chopped green chilies
1 cup sour cream
1 (12 ounce) package shredded Monterey Jack cheese

✪ Preheat oven to 350°.

✪ Sprinkle salt and pepper over beef, brown in large skillet and drain well.

✪ Add taco seasoning mix and 1¼ cups water to beef and simmer 5 minutes.

✪ In another skillet, heat a small amount of oil until hot. Cook tortillas, one at a time, until soft and limp, about 5 to 10 seconds on each side. Drain on paper towels.

✪ Spoon ⅓ cup meat mixture into center of tortilla.

✪ Sprinkle with a little cheddar cheese, roll up and place seam side down into sprayed 9 x 13-inch baking dish.

✪ After filling all tortillas, add enchilada sauce and green chilies to remaining meat mixture. Spoon over tortillas.

✪ Cover and bake for about 30 minutes.

✪ Uncover, spread sour cream over tortillas and sprinkle Monterey Jack cheese over top. Return to oven and cook for about 5 to 10 minutes or until cheese melts. Serves 6 to 8.

★GREEN ENCHILADAS

1½ pounds lean ground beef
1 onion, chopped
1 teaspoon ground cumin
1 teaspoon minced garlic
3 cups shredded longhorn cheese
1 (10 ounce) can cream of chicken soup
¾ cup evaporated milk
1 (7 ounce) can chopped green chilies, drained
1 (2 ounce) jar chopped pimentos
1 (8 ounce) package shredded cheddar cheese
10 to 12 (8 ounce) corn tortillas
Oil

✪ Preheat oven to 350°.

✪ In skillet, brown beef and onion. Add 1 teaspoon salt, cumin and garlic, then add longhorn cheese.

✪ In saucepan, combine soup, milk, green chilies, pimentos and cheddar cheese and heat until cheese melts.

✪ In second skillet, heat a little oil and fry tortillas only enough to soften.

✪ Roll equal amount of meat mixture into each softened tortilla until all meat is used.

✪ Place seam side down in sprayed 9 x 13-inch baking dish. Pour cheese-milk sauce over tortillas.

✪ Bake for 30 to 35 minutes or until hot and bubbly. Serves 6 to 8.

TEXAS TAMALE PIE

1¼ pounds lean ground beef
1 onion, finely chopped
1 (15 ounce) can diced tomatoes
1 (10 ounce) can tomatoes and green chilies
1 (15 ounce) can pinto beans
1 (8 ounce) can whole kernel corn
1 (6 ounce) package cornbread mix
1 teaspoon chili powder

✪ Preheat oven to 375°.

✪ In skillet with a little oil, brown beef and onion. Add tomatoes, tomatoes and green chilies and simmer for about 15 minutes.

✪ Place 3 to 4 tablespoons beans on small plate and mash with fork to thicken beef-tomato mixture slightly. To the beef-tomato mixture, add beans, corn and mashed beans.

✪ Spoon into sprayed 9 x 13-inch glass baking dish.

✪ Mix cornbread mix according to package directions and add extra 2 tablespoons milk for thinner batter. Spoon on top of beef-bean mixture.

✪ Bake for 30 minutes. Serves 6 to 8.

Tamale-vendors were on the squares and street corners of lots of cities and towns in Texas from the turn of the century to about the 1970's and the 1980's.

TAMALE LOAF

3 eggs, beaten
¾ cup milk
1 cup cornmeal
6 tablespoons (¾ stick) butter, melted
1 large onion, finely chopped
2 teaspoons minced garlic
1½ pounds lean ground beef
1 (15 ounce) can stewed tomatoes
1 (10 ounce) can tomatoes and green chilies
1 (15 ounce) can whole kernel corn, drained
2 tablespoons chili powder

✪ Preheat oven to 350°.

✪ In large bowl, combine eggs, milk, cornmeal and melted butter, stir well and set aside.

✪ Brown onion, garlic and ground beef in large skillet. Add tomatoes, tomatoes and green chilies, corn, chili powder and 1 to 2 teaspoons salt and cook on medium heat for about 10 minutes.

✪ Pour into egg-cornmeal mixture and mix well. Pour into sprayed 2- to 3-quart baking dish. Cover and bake for 1 hour. Serves 6 to 8.

★BEEF TACOS

2 pounds ground round steak
¼ cup minced onion
2 cloves garlic, minced
1 tablespoon chili powder
1 teaspoon seasoned salt
1 teaspoon ground cumin
2 jalapenos, seeded, chopped
1 (8 ounce) can tomato sauce
24 taco shells
Shredded lettuce
Finely chopped ripe tomato
Shredded longhorn cheese

✪ Brown meat, add all ingredients except taco shells, lettuce, tomato and cheese. Fill taco shells as desired. Serves 6 to 8.

★ TEXAS-STYLE CHILI RELLENOS

These are mild chili peppers stuffed with meat.

1 pound lean ground beef
Oil
1 onion, minced
2 tablespoons ground coriander
½ teaspoon ground cloves
8 to 10 New Mexico green or red chile peppers
1½ cups flour
½ cup cornmeal
1 teaspoon baking powder
2 eggs
1 cup milk

❂ In heavy skillet brown ground beef with a little oil. Add onion and cook until it is translucent.

❂ Drain excess fat and add ¼ cup water, ½ teaspoon pepper, 1 teaspoon salt, coriander and cloves. Stir well, simmer for about 1 hour or until most of liquid thickens and stir occasionally. Set aside.

❂ Place chile peppers on baking sheet and place under broiler in oven. Roast peppers until the skins blacken. Remove from oven, turn peppers and roast under broiler until all sides are charred.

❂ Remove from oven, cool and remove outer skins of peppers. Stuff peppers with meat mixture.

❂ In medium bowl mix flour, cornmeal, baking powder and pinch of salt. Beat eggs and add to flour mixture. Pour in milk and stir well.

❂ Wrap stuffed peppers in dough and drop into hot oil of deep fryer. Fry until golden brown, drain and serve immediately with salsa. Serves 4 to 6.

CHILE RELLENOS BAKE

1 pound lean ground beef
1 small onion, chopped
2 (4 ounce) cans green chilies, divided
1 (8 ounce) package shredded Mexican 4-cheese blend, divided
1⅔ cups milk
2 tablespoons flour
4 eggs, beaten

✪ Preheat oven to 350°.

✪ In skillet, cook ground beef and onion, drain and add ¾ teaspoon salt
and ½ teaspoon pepper.

✪ Spread 1 can green chilies in sprayed 9 x 13-inch baking dish. Top
with half cheese and then all meat mixture.

✪ Place second can green chilies over meat and add remaining cheese.

✪ Combine about 3 tablespoons milk with flour and mix well. Pour in
remaining milk, ½ teaspoon salt and beaten eggs and mix well.

✪ Pour egg mixture over casserole and bake for 45 to 50 minutes or until
knife inserted in center comes out clean. Cut into squares to serve.
Serves 4 to 6.

The oldest Spanish fort and mission in the U.S. was built in Texas in 1721 and
named Presidio La Bahia and Esperitu Santo Mission.

CHILES RELLENOS MAMACITA

1 (7 ounce) can whole green chilies
1 (8 ounce) package shredded Monterey Jack cheese
1 (8 ounce) package shredded cheddar-colby cheese
2⅓ cups milk
4 eggs, beaten
1 cup baking mix
¾ teaspoon seasoned salt
½ teaspoon seasoned pepper

✪ Preheat oven to 325°. Split chilies, rinse, remove seeds and dry chilies. Place in sprayed 7 x 11-inch baking dish.

✪ Sprinkle both cheeses on top of chilies. Combine, milk, beaten eggs, baking mix, seasoned salt and pepper and mix well. Pour over cheeses, but do not stir.

✪ Bake for 55 minutes or until center is set. Serves 4 to 6.

★BEEF FLAUTAS

2 to 3 cups shredded beef brisket
1 tablespoon chili powder
1 tablespoon snipped cilantro
2 teaspoons cumin
1 onion, chopped
2 cloves garlic, minced
Canola oil
Corn tortillas

✪ Season shredded brisket with chili powder, cilantro, cumin and salt and stir. Mix onion and garlic with beef. Place several tablespoons shredded brisket in corn tortilla and fold up like envelope and secure with toothpick.

✪ Heat oil in deep saucepan and carefully drop flauta into oil. Fry until crispy, remove from oil and drain. Serve hot. Serves 4 to 5.

MEXICAN-BEEF CASSEROLE

Tortilla Chips
Oil
1½ pounds lean ground beef
1 onion, chopped
1 bell pepper, chopped
1 (16 ounce) can Mexican stewed tomatoes
1 (15 ounce) can ranch-style pinto beans with juice
¼ cup salsa
1 (1 ounce) package dry onion soup mix
1 teaspoon seasoned salt
1 teaspoon chili powder
¼ teaspoon garlic powder
½ teaspoon ground coriander
1 (12 ounce) package shredded cheddar cheese

✪ Preheat oven to 350°.

✪ In sprayed 9 x 13-inch baking dish, place about 40 chips on bottom of dish. Crush slightly with your hands.

✪ Place oil in skillet and brown meat, onion and bell pepper.

✪ Add tomatoes, beans, salsa, onion soup mix, salt, chili powder, ¼ teaspoon pepper, garlic powder and coriander and mix well.

✪ Heat and simmer 3 to 4 minutes.

✪ Spoon over chips in baking dish and cover with cheese.

✪ Cover baking dish with foil and bake for 35 minutes. Serves 6 to 8.

Editor's Choice

HOMER'S BEST MARINATED SMOKED CHICKEN

This is smoked chicken at its best!

3 chickens, cut in half
Seasoned pepper
½ cup (1 stick) butter
2 teaspoons Worcestershire sauce
2 dashes hot sauce
2 tablespoons lemon juice
½ teaspoon garlic salt
1 (12 ounce) can lemon-lime carbonated soda

✪ Sprinkle chicken with seasoned pepper and leave at room temperature for 1 hour.

✪ Melt butter with Worcestershire, hot sauce, lemon juice and garlic salt and add lemon-lime carbonated soda.

✪ Cook chickens in smoker with charcoal and mesquite-wood fire. Turn often and baste with butter-lemon mixture several times.

✪ When chicken is done (about 60 minutes) baste once more to keep chicken moist. Serves 8 to 10.

The *Authorized Texas Ranger Cookbook* is filled with recipes from Texas Rangers, past and present. If you cannot visit the Texas Ranger museum in Waco, this cookbook is the next best thing. There are captivating photos of Texas Ranger campsites, Davy Crockett's rifle, Bonnie Parker's shot gun, famous Rangers on horseback, Chief Quannah Parker and exciting Wild West tales from days of the Old West to the last days of Bonnie and Clyde.

BEER-IN-THE-REAR CHICKEN

Straight from The Authorized Texas Ranger Cookbook by Cheryl and Johnny Harris, this recipe captures the spirit and imagination of retired Texas Ranger, Bill Gunn.

1 whole frying chicken
Olive oil
Rosemary
Thyme
Onion flakes
Garlic flakes
Onion, apple or celery slices
Light beer

✪ Buy a whole frying-size chicken. This will work equally well on the BBQ pit or in the kitchen oven . You can prepare the chicken to suit individual tastes. You are limited only by your imagination.

✪ Some suggestions are to rub the chicken with olive oil and sprinkle with rosemary and thyme, or sprinkle with onion flakes and garlic flakes (inside and out). Place slice of onion, apple or celery in cavity of chicken.

✪ After preparing chicken open a can of light beer (removing tab and opening one or two additional holes) and insert can of beer upright into cavity of the chicken and place upright in shallow pan in oven at 325° for 2 hours or until done.

✪ If barbecuing place chicken upright on grill (after placing beer can in cavity). Baste with sauce about 30 minutes before done. Serves 4.

In Cheryl's notes about the recipe, she writes: *"Don't cook just one – there won't be enough to go around! When Bill Gunn first introduced us to this recipe, we had our doubts. We could not imagine it was so easy and sooo good. Before we had a chance to try it out, a friend, Bob Weber, asked us over to eat one night.*

On the pit along with the beef he was cooking were whole chickens which were standing upright on beer cans. They were ready to come off the grill before the beef. He had slit the skins and put seeded quarters of jalapenos between the skin and meat. Then he had rubbed dry Hidden Valley dressing mix all over the chicken for seasoning and set each chicken on a can of beer on the pit. It was some of the best chicken we have ever eaten."

TEXAS-PECAN CHICKEN

1 cup buttermilk
1 egg, beaten
1 cup flour
1 cup very finely grated pecans and ¼ cup chopped pecans
2 tablespoons sesame seeds
2 teaspoons paprika
6 to 8 boneless, skinless, chicken breast halves
¼ cup (½ stick) butter

✪ Preheat oven to 350°.

✪ In shallow bowl, combine buttermilk and egg. In larger shallow bowl, combine flour, grated pecans, sesame seeds, paprika, 1 teaspoon salt and ¼ teaspoon pepper.

✪ Dip chicken breasts in egg-milk mixture, then coat well in flour-pecan mixture.

✪ Melt butter in sprayed 9 x 13-inch baking pan and place breaded chicken in pan. Sprinkle chopped pecans over chicken breasts.

✪ Bake for 30 to 35 minutes or until flour mixture is light brown. Serves 6 to 8.

TIP: **To make buttermilk, mix 1 cup milk with 1 tablespoon lemon juice or vinegar and let milk rest for about 10 minutes.**

The largest spur manufacturer in the U.S. is located in Bandera, the Cowboy Capital of the World.

TORTILLA-CHIP CHICKEN

4 to 5 boneless, skinless chicken breast halves
1 (10 ounce) package tortilla chips, divided
1 onion, chopped
3 ribs celery, chopped
1 (10 ounce) can cream of chicken soup
2 (10 ounce) cans tomatoes and green chilies
1 (16 ounce) package cubed Velveeta® cheese

✪ Preheat oven to 350°.

✪ In large saucepan, boil chicken breasts in water about 30 minutes or until chicken is tender. Cool, cut into small bite-sized pieces and set aside.

✪ Place half chips in sprayed 9 x 13-inch baking dish. Crush a little with your hand.

✪ In large saucepan, combine onion, celery, chicken soup, tomatoes and green chilies, and Velveeta cheese. On medium heat, stir until cheese melts. Add chicken pieces and pour over chips.

✪ Crush remaining chips in plastic bag with rolling pin. Sprinkle over chicken-cheese mixture.

✪ Bake for about 35 minutes or until bubbly around edges. Serves 6 to 8.

The Lady Bird Johnson Wildflower Center was established in 1982 for research and preservation of native Texas plants and has more than 180 acres of wildflowers.

THREE CHEERS FOR CHICKEN

6 to 8 boneless, skinless chicken breasts halves
6 tablespoons (¾ stick) butter
1 onion, chopped
½ bell pepper, chopped
1 (2 ounce) jar chopped pimento
1 cup uncooked rice
1 (10 ounce) can cream of chicken soup
1 (10 ounce) can cream of celery soup
1 (8 ounce) can sliced water chestnuts
1 (8 ounce) package shredded cheddar cheese

✪ Preheat oven to 350°.

✪ Salt and pepper chicken and place in large 11 x 15-inch glass baking dish.

✪ Melt butter and add onion, bell pepper, pimentos, rice, soups, 2 soup cans water and water chestnuts and pour over chicken breasts. Bake for 15 minutes.

✪ Turn oven to 325° and cook 55 minutes more.

✪ Add cheese, return to oven for the last 5 minutes. Serves 6 to 8.

More bird species can be found in the Big Bend National Park than in any other national park in the U.S. More than half of all bird species in the U.S. are in the park.

★TEXAS CHICKEN FAJITAS

6 to 8 boneless, skinless chicken breast halves
Flour tortillas

MARINADE:
1 cup salsa
1 cup bottled Italian dressing
2 tablespoons lemon juice
2 tablespoons chopped green onions
1 teaspoon garlic powder
1 teaspoon celery salt

FILLING FOR FAJITAS:
Salsa
Guacamole
Grilled onions
Grilled bell peppers
Chopped tomatoes
Shredded cheese
Sour cream

✪ Combine all marinade ingredients and 1 teaspoon pepper. Mix well.

✪ Remove any fat from meat, wipe dry with paper towels and place meat in shallow baking dish.

✪ Pour marinade over meat and marinate overnight or at least 6 hours in refrigerator.

✪ Drain liquid and cook over hot charcoal.

✪ Cut meat diagonally. Place a few strips meat on warmed, flour tortilla, select fillings and roll-up to eat. Serves 4 to 6.

OVEN-FRIED CHICKEN

1 medium fryer chicken, cut into serving pieces
1 (1 ounce) envelope ranch buttermilk salad dressing mix
1 cup buttermilk
½ cup mayonnaise
2 to 3 cups crushed corn flakes

✪ Preheat oven to 350°. Pat chicken pieces dry and place on paper towels.

✪ In shallow bowl, combine ranch dressing mix, buttermilk and mayonnaise and mix well.

✪ Dip chicken pieces in dressing and cover well. Roll each piece in corn flakes and coat all sides well.

✪ Arrange pieces so they do not touch in sprayed 9 x 13-inch baking dish. Bake for 1 hour. If chicken pieces are not brown, cook another 15 minutes. Serves 6 to 8.

SUNDAY-CHICKEN CASSEROLE

5 boneless, skinless chicken breast halves, cooked, cubed
2 (8 ounce) cartons sour cream
1 (7 ounce) package uncooked, ready-cut spaghetti
2 (10 ounce) cans cream of chicken soup
1 (4 ounce) can mushrooms, drained
½ cup (1 stick) butter, melted
1 (8 ounce) package fresh, grated parmesan cheese

✪ Preheat oven to 325°. Combine chicken, sour cream, spaghetti, chicken soup, mushrooms, butter and ⅛ teaspoon pepper.

✪ Pour into sprayed 9 x 13-inch baking dish. Sprinkle cheese on top. Bake, covered, for 50 minutes. Serves 6 to 8.

SOUTH-OF-THE-BORDER CHICKEN

5 to 6 boneless, skinless chicken breast halves
1 (8 ounce) package shredded Monterey Jack cheese
1 (4 ounce) can chopped green chilies
1 teaspoon cilantro
3 tablespoons dehydrated onion
6 tablespoons (¾ stick) butter
2 teaspoons cumin
1 teaspoon chili powder
Tortilla chips, crushed

✪ Preheat oven to 350°.

✪ Pound chicken breasts flat. In bowl, mix cheese, chilies, cilantro and onion.

✪ Place 2 to 3 tablespoons cheese mixture on each chicken breast, roll up and place seam side down in large, sprayed casserole.

✪ In saucepan, melt butter, add cumin and chili powder and spoon over chicken.

✪ Bake covered for 45 minutes. Uncover and top with crushed chips. Return to oven and bake for an additional 10 to 15 minutes. Serves 4 to 6.

Texas is the largest producer of upland cotton in the U.S.

Texas is the largest producer of grain sorghum in the U.S.

CHICKEN-TACO BAKE

12 tortillas
Oil
1 onion, chopped
2 tablespoons butter
2 cups tomato juice
1 (4 ounce) can chopped green chilies
1 (12 ounce) package shredded cheddar cheese
1 (8 ounce) carton whipping cream
5 chicken breasts, boiled, cut into bite-size pieces

✪ Quarter tortillas and fry until crisp. Drain and set aside.

✪ Saute onion in butter; add tomato juice, ½ teaspoon salt, ½ teaspoon pepper and green chilies. Simmer for 30 minutes.

✪ Add cheese, cream and chicken; heat until cheese melts.

✪ Alternate layers of chicken-cheese mixture and tortillas in sprayed 9 x 13-inch baking dish.

✪ Allow to set for 2 to 3 hours. Bake at 350° for 30 to 35 minutes. Serves 6 to 8.

The world's largest equine registry is at the American Quarter Horse Headquarters in Amarillo.

CILANTRO CHICKEN

1 teaspoon seasoned salt
2 teaspoons seasoned pepper, divided
2 teaspoons cilantro
1 teaspoon cumin
6 to 8 boneless, skinless chicken breast halves
2 cups cracker crumbs
Oil
3 tablespoons butter
¼ cup flour
¼ teaspoon cumin
1 teaspoon cilantro
2 cups milk
⅓ cup dry white wine
1 (8 ounce) package shredded Monterey Jack cheese

✪ Preheat oven to 350°.

✪ Mix seasoned salt, 1 teaspoon seasoned pepper, cilantro and cumin.
Sprinkle over chicken breasts and dip in cracker crumbs.

✪ Pour a little oil in large skillet and brown chicken. Transfer to sprayed
10 x 15-inch baking dish.

✪ In saucepan, melt butter, blend in flour, ½ teaspoon salt, 1 teaspoon
seasoned pepper, cumin and cilantro. Add milk, stirring constantly,
and cook until it thickens.

✪ Remove from heat, stir in wine and pour sauce over chicken. Bake for
45 minutes.

✪ Remove from oven and sprinkle cheese on top of each piece of
chicken. Return to oven for 5 minutes. Serves 8.

★KING RANCH CHICKEN

The King Ranch is the largest ranch in the U.S. and was established in 1853 from a Spanish land grant. Today the ranch covers more than 800,000 acres in South Texas with additional holdings in Brazil and 3 states in the U.S.

8 (8 inch) corn tortillas, divided
Chicken broth
2 tablespoons butter
1 onion, chopped
1 green bell pepper, chopped
1 (14 ounce) can cream of chicken soup
1 (14 ounce) can cream of mushroom soup
1 tablespoon chili powder
3 to 4 pound fryer, cooked, boned, diced
1 (12 ounce) package shredded cheese
1 (10 ounce) can chopped tomatoes and green chilies

✪ Preheat oven to 350°.

✪ In sprayed 10 x 15-inch baking pan, layer half tortillas dipped in hot chicken broth just long enough to soften.

✪ In skillet with butter, saute onion and bell pepper. Stir in soups, chili powder and diced chicken.

✪ Pour layer of half soup-chicken mixture over tortillas and half cheese. Repeat layers and pour tomatoes and green chilies over casserole.

✪ Bake for 40 to 45 minutes or until hot and bubbly. Serves 6 to 8.

The Amon Carter Museum of Western Art in Fort Worth is the finest collection and most complete group of works by Frederic Remington and Charles M. Russell.

FIESTA CHICKEN

½ cup (1 stick) butter
2 cups finely crushed cheese crackers
1 (1 ounce) envelope taco seasoning mix
5 to 6 boneless, skinless, chicken breast halves, flattened
1 bunch fresh green onions with tops, chopped
1 teaspoon dry chicken bouillon
1 pint whipping cream
1 (8 ounce) package shredded Monterey Jack cheese
1 (4 ounce) can chopped green chilies

✪ Preheat oven to 350°.

✪ Melt butter in large baking dish and set aside.

✪ Combine cracker crumbs and taco mix. Dredge chicken in crumb mixture and pat mixture well to use all cracker crumbs.

✪ Place chicken breasts in baking dish with melted butter.

✪ In saucepan, take out several tablespoons melted butter and place in saucepan. Add onion and saute.

✪ Turn heat off, add chicken bouillon and stir. Add whipping cream, cheese and chopped green chilies and mix well. Pour over chicken in baking dish.

✪ Bake uncovered for 55 minutes. Serves 4 to 6.

The XIT Ranch, located in West Texas, was the largest fenced ranch in the world with more than 1,500 miles of fence. There were more than 150,000 head of cattle, 100 dams, 325 windmills and 94 pastures.

The largest private herd of registered Texas Longhorns in the world can be found on the YO Ranch in the Kerrville, Texas area. The Texas Longhorn is the Official Large Mammal of the State of Texas.

Editor's Choice

★CHICKEN-FRIED CHICKEN AND CREAM GRAVY

1 medium fryer chicken, cut up
2 eggs, beaten
2 tablespoons milk
Flour
Oil or shortening

GRAVY:
3 tablespoons flour
1 to 1½ cups milk

✪ Sprinkle salt and pepper over each piece of chicken. Add milk to beaten eggs and dip chicken into egg mixture. Roll in flour and coat chicken well.

✪ Heat about ¼ inch oil or shortening in heavy skillet and brown chicken on both sides. Lower heat and cook until tender, about 25 minutes.

✪ For gravy, remove chicken from skillet and add 3 tablespoons flour and ½ teaspoon each of salt and pepper.

✪ Turn burner to high heat and add milk, stirring constantly, until gravy thickens. Serves 4 to 5.

The southern part of the Texas coastline is one of the premier bird-watching areas in the U.S. Padre Island is a key stopping point for migratory species traveling from Canada and Central America and is the northern boundary for some Central American species.

JAZZY CHICKEN AND DRESSING

1 (8 ounce) package stuffing
3 cups diced, cooked chicken
1 (15 ounce) can golden hominy, drained
1 (4 ounce) can chopped green chilies, drained
½ cup chopped red bell pepper
2 tablespoons dried parsley flakes
1 (10 ounce) can cream of chicken soup
1 (8 ounce) carton sour cream
¼ cup (½ stick) butter, melted
2 teaspoons ground cumin
1 (8 ounce) package shredder Monterey Jack cheese

✪ Preheat oven to 350°.

✪ In large mixing bowl, combine ½ cup water, ½ teaspoon salt and all ingredients except cheese.

✪ Mix well and pour into sprayed 9 x 13-inch baking dish and cover with foil. Bake for 35 minutes.

✪ Uncover and sprinkle with cheese. Bake for an additional 5 minutes. Serves 6 to 8.

The Aransas National Wildlife Refuge is the only place in the U.S. where more than half of the U.S. population of the near-extinct whooping crane spends winters. The whooping crane is the largest bird in America with a wing span of more than 7 feet and a height of 5 feet.

"MILD" CHICKEN PEPE

1 (10½ ounce) can cream of mushroom soup
1 (10½ ounce) can cream of chicken soup
1 cup milk
1 (1 ounce) envelope taco seasoning
1 onion, chopped
½ teaspoon celery salt
1 (4 ounce) can chopped green chilies
5 to 6 boneless, skinless chicken breasts, cooked
1 (12 ounce) package shredded cheddar cheese
1 (16 ounce) package shredded Monterey Jack cheese
1 (10 ounce) package corn tortillas or chips

✪ Preheat oven to 325°.

✪ Combine soups, milk, taco seasoning, onion, celery salt and green chilies.

✪ Cut chicken breasts in bite-size pieces. Combine cheeses.

✪ In sprayed 9 x 13-inch glass baking dish, layer the following twice: chips, chicken, soup mixture and cheese.

✪ Bake uncovered for 1 hour. Serves 6 to 8.

The Brazoria National Wildlife Refuge covers more than 43,000 acres of coastal Texas and protects coastal wetlands for migratory birds and other wildlife.

GOURMET CHICKEN

2 medium skinless chickens, quartered
Flour
Oil
1 (16 ounce) can sliced pineapple with juice
1 cup sugar
3 tablespoons cornstarch
¾ cup vinegar
1 tablespoon soy sauce
¼ teaspoon ground ginger
2 chicken bouillon cubes
1 tablespoon lemon juice
2 bell peppers, cut in strips
Cooked rice

✪ Preheat oven to 350°.

✪ Wash chicken and pat dry with paper towel.

✪ Coat chicken with a little salt and pepper and flour. Brown chicken quarters in oil and place in large shallow roasting pan.

✪ To make sauce, drain pineapple syrup into 2-cup measure. Add water (or orange juice) to make 1½ cups.

✪ In medium saucepan, combine sugar, cornstarch, pineapple syrup, vinegar, soy sauce, ginger, bouillon cubes and lemon juice and bring to boil.

✪ Stir constantly for about 2 minutes or until sauce thickens and becomes clear. Pour over browned chicken.

✪ Bake covered for about 40 minutes.

✪ Place pineapple slices and bell pepper on top of chicken and bake for 10 to 15 minutes longer. Serve on fluffy white rice. Serves 8.

BARBECUED CHICKEN

1 (2 pound) fryer, quartered
½ cup ketchup
¼ cup butter (½ stick), melted
2 tablespoons sugar
1 tablespoon prepared mustard
½ teaspoon minced garlic
¼ cup lemon juice
¼ cup white vinegar
¼ cup Worcestershire sauce
Several dashes hot pepper sauce, optional

✪ Preheat oven to 325°. Sprinkle chicken quarters with salt and pepper and brown in skillet. Place in large sprayed baking pan.

✪ Combine ketchup, butter, sugar, mustard, garlic, lemon juice, vinegar Worcestershire and hot pepper sauce. Pour over chicken. Cover and bake for 50 minutes. Serves 4.

FAVORITE CHICKEN

8 boneless, skinless chicken breast halves
1 (8 ounce) bottle Catalina dressing
1 (1 ounce) envelope dry onion soup mix
1 (8 ounce) jar apricot preserves
1 tablespoon lime juice
Cooked rice

✪ Preheat oven to 325°. Place chicken breasts in sprayed 9 x 13-inch baking dish.

✪ In saucepan, combine Catalina dressing, soup mix, apricot preserves and lime juice. Heat just enough to mix.

✪ Pour over chicken breasts and bake covered for 1 hour 10 minutes. Serve over hot rice. Serves 8.

★FRIED CHICKEN LIVERS

1 pound chicken livers, washed, dried
2 tablespoons buttermilk
2 eggs, beaten
Flour
Oil

✪ Season chicken livers with pepper. Add buttermilk to beaten eggs and dip livers into egg mixture. Roll in flour and coat livers well.

✪ Heat about ¼ inch oil in heavy skillet and brown livers on both sides. Lower heat and cook until tender, about 15 to 20 minutes.

✪ Remove from skillet, drain on paper towels, sprinkle salt and pepper again and serve immediately. Serves 4.

TIP: To make buttermilk, mix 1 cup milk with 1 tablespoon lemon juice or vinegar and let milk rest for about 10 minutes.

EASY-OVEN CHICKEN
One step does all!

6 tablespoons (¾ stick) butter
1 cup uncooked rice
1 (1 ounce) package dry onion soup mix
1 cup chopped celery
1 (14 ounce) can chicken broth
1 (10 ounce) can cream of chicken soup
1 teaspoon seasoned pepper
8 boneless, skinless chicken breast halves

✪ Preheat oven to 325°. Melt butter in 9 x 13-inch glass baking dish. Add 2 cups water and all remaining ingredients, except chicken.

✪ Lay chicken breasts on rice and liquid mixture and cover with foil. Bake for 1 hour 10 minutes. Serves 6 to 8.

★SOUR CREAM CHICKEN ENCHILADAS

4 to 5 boneless, skinless chicken breast halves
1 onion, chopped
2 tablespoons butter
1 (4 ounce) can chopped green chilies
1 (12 ounce) package shredded cheddar cheese
2 teaspoons chili powder, divided
1 (16 ounce) carton sour cream, divided
10 to 12 flour tortillas
¼ cup flour
¼ cup (½ stick) butter, melted
1 (12 ounce) package shredded Monterey Jack cheese, divided

✪ In saucepan, cook chicken in enough water to cover chicken, drain and reserve 1½ cups broth. Allow chicken to cool and chop into small pieces.

✪ Saute onion in butter, add chicken, green chilies, cheddar cheese, 1 teaspoon chili powder and 1 cup sour cream and mix well.

✪ Microwave tortillas on high for about 1 minute or until softened.

✪ Spoon chicken-cheese mixture onto tortillas and roll up to enclose filling.

✪ Place seam-side down in sprayed 10 x 15-inch baking pan.

✪ In saucepan, combine flour and melted butter, mix well and add reserved broth; cook stirring constantly until thick and bubbly.

✪ Fold in one-half Monterey Jack cheese, remaining sour cream and remaining chili powder; spoon over enchiladas.

✪ Bake at 350° for 30 minutes. Remove from oven and sprinkle with remaining Monterey Jack cheese. Serves 8 to 10.

 *Editor's Choice*

CREAMY TURKEY ENCHILADAS

This is great for leftover turkey after the holidays.

2 tablespoons butter
1 onion, finely chopped
3 fresh green onions, chopped
½ teaspoon garlic powder
½ teaspoon seasoned salt
1 (7 ounce) can chopped green chilies
2 (8 ounce) packages cream cheese, softened
3 cups finely diced turkey breasts or chicken
8 (8 inch) flour tortillas
2 (8 ounce) cartons whipping cream
1 (16 ounce) package shredded Monterey Jack cheese

✪ Preheat oven to 325°.

✪ In large skillet, add butter and saute onions. Add garlic powder, seasoned salt and green chilies.

✪ Stir in cream cheese, heat and stir until cream cheese melts. Add diced turkey.

✪ Lay out 8 tortillas and spoon about 3 heaping tablespoons turkey mixture on each tortilla. (Use all turkey mixture.)

✪ Roll up tortillas and place seam side down in lightly sprayed 10 x 15-inch baking pan. Pour whipping cream over enchiladas and sprinkle cheese over top.

✪ Bake uncovered for 30 to 35 minutes. (Do not let cheese brown.) Serve with large spatula so enchiladas do not break up. Serves 6 to 8.

JALAPENO TURKEY

2 small onions, chopped
3 tablespoons butter
1 (10 ounce) package frozen chopped spinach, cooked, drained
5 jalapenos peppers or 1 (7 ounce) can chopped green chilies
1 (8 ounce) carton sour cream
2 (10 ounce) cans chicken soup
1 (13 ounce) package tortilla chips, slightly crushed
4 cups diced turkey breasts or chicken
1 (12 ounce) package shredded Monterey Jack cheese

✪ Preheat oven to 350°. In skillet, saute onion in butter. Blend in spinach, peppers, sour cream, soups and ½ teaspoon salt.

✪ In sprayed 10 x 15-inch baking dish or 2 (9 x 9-inch) dishes, alternate tortillas, turkey, spinach mixture and cheese. Repeat layers with cheese on top. Bake for 35 minutes. Serves 8 to 10.

★TURKEY JERKY

Turkey breasts, cooked
Salt or seasoned salt
Freshly ground black pepper

✪ Preheat oven to 175°. Slice turkey breasts across the grain in very thin slices about ¼ inch thick.

✪ Place on baking sheet and sprinkle both sides lightly with salt and a lot of freshly ground black pepper.

✪ Cook in oven until turkey gets to the right consistency. It should be very dense, dark brown, but not burned. (The time is different with the size of pieces. Beef jerky takes 6 to 8 hours or more, but turkey jerky usually takes less time. Adjust times according to taste.)

RANCH PORK CHOPS

6 to 8 boneless pork chops
2 tablespoons oil
1 cup chili sauce
1 (10 ounce) can tomatoes and green chilies
½ cup plum jelly
½ (1 ounce) envelope ranch dressing mix
1 bunch fresh green onions with tops, chopped
1 teaspoon minced garlic

✪ Preheat oven to 325°.

✪ In skillet, brown pork chops in oil and place in sprayed 9 x 13-inch baking pan.

✪ In same skillet, combine chili sauce, tomatoes, chilies, jelly, dressing mix, green onions and garlic.

✪ Bring mixture to boil and simmer 5 minutes. Pour over pork chops and bake for 55 minutes. Serves 6 to 8.

YEE-HA PORK CHOPS

1 (1 ounce) envelope taco seasoning
4 (½ inch) boneless pork loin chops
1 tablespoon oil
Salsa

✪ Rub taco seasoning over pork chops. In skillet, brown pork chops in oil over medium heat.

✪ Add 2 tablespoons water, turn heat to low and simmer pork chops about 40 minutes. (Check to see if water should be added.) Spoon salsa over pork chops to serve. Serves 4.

PORK CHOP-CHEDDAR BAKE

8 pork chops
1 (10½ ounce) can cream of mushroom soup
1 cup rice
1 (12 ounce) package shredded cheddar cheese, divided
2 tablespoons minced onion
2 tablespoons bell pepper, chopped
1 (4 ounce) can sliced mushrooms, drained
½ teaspoon seasoned salt
1 (6 ounce) can french-fried onions

✪ Preheat oven to 325°.

✪ Brown pork chops lightly. Drain and put in sprayed 9 x 13-inch glass baking dish.

✪ Mix soup, 2 cups water, rice, ¾ cup cheese, onion, bell pepper, mushrooms, seasoned salt and ½ teaspoon pepper and pour over pork chops. Cover with foil and bake for 1 hour 15 minutes.

✪ Uncover and top with remaining cheese and french-fried onions. Return to oven until cheese melts. Serves 6 to 8.

"Between 1850 and 1920 thousands of Czechs left their homes in Moravia and Bohemia to come to Texas in search of a better life. Today you can visit towns like Fayetteville, Praha and Hallettsville where the Czech language is in everyday use."

The Melting Pot: Ethnic Cuisine in Texas
The Institute of Texan Cultures of The University of Texas at San Antonio

Mexican Pork Tenderloin with Zucchini

2 pounds pork tenderloin, cubed
1 small onion, diced
1 green bell pepper, diced
2 cloves garlic, minced
1 teaspoon ground cumin
3 tomatoes, diced
1½ pounds Mexican squash or zucchini, cubed
1 (15 ounce) can whole kernel corn

✪ In large skillet, brown pork over medium heat and add onion and bell pepper. Cover and cook on low for 15 minutes.

✪ Add garlic, cumin and tomatoes and cook another 10 minutes.

✪ Add squash and cook, covered, for 30 minutes. Add corn and 1 teaspoon salt. Simmer 30 minutes. Serves 6 to 8.

"The Czechs who came to Texas brought their religion, their language, their folklore and their preferences in food. In time many of the old customs were altered or disappeared, but Czech Texans are still known for their delicious food. Today a typical menu might include soup, baked pork loin, sauerkraut boiled potatoes and kolaches for dessert."

The Melting Pot: Ethnic Cuisine in Texas
The Institute of Texan Cultures of The University of Texas at San Antonio

MARINATED PORK LOIN

MARINADE:

⅔ cup soy sauce
⅔ cup oil
3 tablespoons crystallized ginger, minced
2 tablespoons lime juice
1 teaspoon garlic powder

1 (5 to 6 pound) pork loin or pork tenderloin
1 (12 ounce) bottle chili sauce
1 (16 ounce) jar apricot preserves

✪ Mix marinade and pour into large plastic bag. Add pork loin and marinate for 24 to 36 hours, turning several times.

✪ Preheat oven to 325°.

✪ Place pork loin and marinade in roaster and cook for about 3 hours.

✪ Mix chili sauce and apricot preserves and pour over pork loin. Return to oven for about 20 minutes. Let pork loin rest for about 20 minutes before slicing. Serves 8 to 10.

Texas is the first state to enter the United States as a sovereign nation. The Republic of Texas entered the U.S. in 1845, three years before California entered the U.S.

Texas is the largest of the 48 contiguous states in the U.S.

 *Editor's Choice*

PRIZE-WINNING PORK TENDERLOIN

MARINADE:

⅔ cup soy sauce
⅔ cup oil
2 tablespoons crystallized ginger, finely chopped
2 tablespoons real lime juice
1 teaspoon garlic powder
2 tablespoons minced onion
2 pork tenderloins

✪ Combine all ingredients in marinade and pour over pork tenderloins. Marinate about 36 hours.

✪ When ready to serve, cook over charcoal fire about 45 minutes. Serves 8 to 10.

★TEXAS SPARERIBS

4 to 5 pounds pork spareribs
¾ cup ketchup
¼ cup lemon juice
⅓ cup packed brown sugar
1 tablespoon Worcestershire sauce
½ teaspoon ground allspice
1½ teaspoons garlic powder
1 teaspoon minced green onion
1 teaspoon seasoned pepper

✪ Place ribs in sprayed 9 x 13-inch baking dish. Mix all other ingredients and 1 teaspoon salt and pour over ribs. Cover and refrigerate 24 hours.

✪ Cook at 350° for about 1 hour. Lower heat to 200° and cook for about 3 hours. Turn ribs once while baking and baste with sauce. Serves 6 to 8.

★SMOKED BABY-BACK OR COUNTRY-STYLE RIBS

The simplicity of this is unbelievable and the flavor is outstanding!

6 to 8 racks baby-back or country-style ribs
Salt
Pepper
Sugar

✪ Lay out racks of ribs on baking sheets and season with salt and pepper thoroughly.

✪ Sprinkle one-third amount of sugar to salt and pepper. Rub in seasonings and set aside for about 30 minutes.

✪ Use charcoal with water-soaked, mesquite or hickory wood chips or mesquite, hickory or oak wood fire and burn to ash-colored without strong flame.

✪ Place ribs on grill away from direct fire and cook with heat and smoke of wood. Add wood chips every hour or so. Cook for about 4 to 5 hours.

✪ Outside of ribs should be caramelized and crusty, but ribs should be moist. Serves 10 to 12.

TIP: **Use barbecue sauce if you particularly like sauce. The slightly sweet, spicy taste of barbecue sauce is surpassed by this simple combination of salt, pepper and sugar when cooked correctly.**

The world's largest masonry structure and the world's tallest column is the San Jacinto Monument. It is 20 feet higher than the Washington Monument.

Editor's Choice

★HAM AND RED-EYE GRAVY

Ham steak, ⅓-inch thick
1 tablespoon oil
½ onion, finely minced
½ teaspoon minced garlic
1 tablespoon cornstarch
1 (10 ounce) can beef broth
⅓ cup strong coffee

✪ Cut ham steak in serving-size pieces. In heavy skillet, brown and cook ham on both sides. Transfer from skillet to serving plate.

✪ In same skillet, combine onion, garlic, cornstarch, beef broth and coffee and cook on low heat until mixture thickens slightly.

✪ To serve, pour gravy over ham, biscuits, mashed potatoes or grits. Serves 3 to 4.

PRALINE HAM

2 (½ inch thick) ham slices, cooked
½ cup maple syrup
3 tablespoons brown sugar
1 tablespoon butter
⅓ cup chopped pecans

✪ Preheat oven to 325°.

✪ Bake ham slices in shallow pan for about 10 minutes. Bring syrup, sugar and butter to boil in small saucepan and stir often.

✪ Stir in pecans and spoon over ham. Bake for another 20 minutes. Serves 4.

APRICOT-BAKED HAM

1 (12 to 15 pound) whole ham, bone-in, fully cooked
Whole cloves
2 tablespoons dry mustard
1¼ cups apricot jam
1¼ cups packed light brown sugar

✪ Preheat oven to 450°.

✪ Trim skin and excess fat from ham. Place ham on rack in large
roasting pan.

✪ Insert whole cloves in ham every inch or so. Be sure to push cloves
into ham surface as far as they will go.

✪ Combine dry mustard and apricot jam and spread over surface of ham.
Pat brown sugar over jam.

✪ Turn oven to 325° and bake uncovered for 15 minutes per pound.

✪ A sugary crust forms on ham and keeps juices inside.

✪ When ham is tender, remove from oven, allow ham to rest for 20
minutes and remove from pan to carve. Serves 10 to 12.

Midland-Odessa is in the middle of the Permian Basin, the richest oil field in
the U.S.

SAUCY HAM LOAF

The sweet and hot mustard is also excellent with sandwiches.

1 pound ground ham
½ pound ground beef
½ pound ground pork
2 eggs
1 cup breadcrumbs or cracker crumbs
2 teaspoons Worcestershire sauce
1 (5 ounce) can evaporated milk
3 tablespoons chili sauce
1 teaspoon seasoned salt
1 teaspoon seasoned pepper
3 bacon slices, optional

SWEET AND HOT MUSTARD SAUCE:
4 ounces dry mustard
1 cup vinegar
3 eggs, beaten
1 cup sugar

✪ Preheat oven to 350°.

✪ Mix all ingredients except bacon and Sweet and Hot Mustard Sauce ingredients. Form into loaf and put in sprayed 9 x 13-inch baking pan.

✪ Place bacon slices on top and bake for 1 hour.

✪ To make Sweet and Hot Mustard, mix mustard and vinegar until smooth and let stand overnight.

✪ Add eggs and sugar and cook in double boiler 8 to 10 minutes or until it coats spoon. Cool and store in covered jars in refrigerator. Serve with ham loaf. Serves 6 to 8.

TIP: Have butcher grind ham, beef and pork.

GRILLED PORK TAMALES

12 to 24 fresh pork tamales with husks
Salsa

✪ Lay tamales with husks on charcoal grill and cook until grill marks show.

✪ Turn tamales and cook until grill marks show on opposite side. Serve with salsa. Serves 8 to 12.

CORPUS GRILLED LEMON SHRIMP

½ cup (1 stick) butter
2 tablespoons Worcestershire sauce
½ teaspoon minced garlic
½ teaspoon celery salt
2 tablespoons lemon juice
2 to 2½ pounds shelled shrimp, drained

✪ In saucepan, melt butter and add Worcestershire, garlic, celery salt and lemon juice.

✪ Place shrimp in bowl and pour butter mixture over shrimp. Marinate at room temperature for about 2 hours.

✪ Grill shrimp for about 3 to 5 minutes (according to size) and baste with butter mixture. Shrimp will turn pink when done. Serves 4 to 5.

Shrimp Cooked in Beer

2 pounds shrimp
2 cans beer
3 tablespoons pickling spice
Lemon slices

✪ In large saucepan or stew pot, pour beer in pot and turn on high heat.

✪ Add pickling spice, lemon slices and ½ teaspoon salt. When mixture is steaming, add shrimp and stir well. Make sure there is enough liquid to cover or almost cover shrimp.

✪ Cook just until shrimp turns pink, remove from pot and drain. Serves 4 to 6.

TIP: For larger amounts, use 1½ to 2 tablespoons pickling spice per pound and enough beer to cover shrimp.

Barbecued Shrimp Jose

2 (8 ounce) cans tomato sauce
1 cup corn oil
⅓ cup red wine vinegar
2 tablespoons ketchup
2 cloves garlic, minced
¼ cup minced cilantro
1 teaspoon freshly ground black pepper
18 to 22 shrimp

✪ Combine tomato sauce, oil, red wine vinegar and ketchup and mix well. Stir in garlic, cilantro, oregano, 2 teaspoons salt and ground black pepper and mix well.

✪ Add shrimp, cover with barbecue sauce and refrigerate for at least 2 to 3 hours. Stir shrimp to coat with sauce several times while marinating.

✪ Put shrimp in 9 x 13-inch baking dish, place under broiler and cook 3 to 5 minutes per side or until light brown. Serve immediately. Serves 4.

GALVESTON ISLAND STUFFED CRAB

¼ bell pepper, finely diced
1 small onion, finely diced
2 ribs celery, finely diced
¼ cup (½ stick) butter
8 ounces lump crabmeat
1 tablespoon white wine Worcestershire sauce
1 tablespoon ketchup
1 (8 ounce) carton whipping cream
1 cup seasoned breadcrumbs

✪ Preheat oven to 350°.

✪ Saute pepper, onion and celery in butter and set aside.

✪ In bowl, combine remaining ingredients and add onion-celery mixture. Spoon into crab shells and bake for 30 to 35 minutes. Serves 4.

DEEP-FRIED SHRIMP

1 cup milk
2 eggs, beaten
1½ cups flour
2 teaspoons seasoned salt
1 to 1½ pounds medium shrimp, peeled, veined
About 40 saltine crackers, heavily crushed
Oil
Prepared cocktail sauce

✪ In shallow bowl, combine milk and eggs. In another shallow bowl, combine flour and seasoned salt.

✪ Dip shrimp in flour mixture, then in milk-egg mixture and finally in cracker crumbs. Make sure crumbs cover shrimp well.

✪ Deep-fry shrimp until golden brown and serve with cocktail sauce. Serves 4.

Port Aransas Stuffed Flounder

½ cup (1 stick) butter
1 pound fresh or frozen crabmeat, thawed
½ onion, finely minced
½ cup chopped fresh parsley
4 green onions, finely chopped
1 teaspoon lemon juice
2 (4 ounce) cans sliced mushrooms, drained
2 cups prepared seasoned breadcrumbs
2 eggs, beaten
¼ teaspoon cayenne pepper
6 to 8 fresh flounder with large pocket cut by butcher
½ cup (1 stick) butter, melted
½ cup dry white wine

✪ Preheat oven to 375°.

✪ In saucepan, melt butter and add crabmeat, onion, parsley and onions. Cook on medium heat about 5 to 10 minutes or until onions are translucent.

✪ Add lemon juice and mushrooms. Stir in breadcrumbs, eggs, a little salt and pepper, and cayenne pepper and mix well. Open flounder pockets and fill with crab stuffing.

✪ Arrange flounder on sprayed large baking pan. Combine remaining butter and white wine and baste flounder. Bake for 15 minutes.

✪ Lower oven heat to 300°, baste again with butter-wine mixture and bake for an additional 15 to 20 minutes. Serves 8 to 10.

GRILLED SWORDFISH WITH CILANTRO-CITRUS SAUCE

If you can find Texas Ruby Red Grapefruit, it is great in this recipe.

3 large Texas Ruby Red Grapefruit
3 cloves garlic, minced
2 teaspoons chili powder
2 teaspoons ground cumin
½ cup oil
¼ cup white wine
3 fresh mild jalapenos
4 to 5 (1 inch) swordfish steaks
¼ cup snipped cilantro
2 teaspoons butter

✪ In 4-cup measuring cup squeeze grapefruit to measure ¾ to 1 cup juice. Peel remaining grapefruit, split into sections and refrigerate until ready to use.

✪ Add garlic, chili powder, cumin, 1 teaspoon salt, vegetable oil and white wine to grapefruit juice and mix.

✪ Slice jalapenos, remove seeds and ribs and chop. Add to marinade ingredients, mix well and reserve ⅓ cup.

✪ Place swordfish steaks in flat, glass dish and pour marinade over steaks. Cover dish and refrigerate about 1 hour.

✪ Prepare charcoal or wood fire and grate. Before grilling, pour about ½ cup marinade from swordfish dish into small saucepan. Add jalapenos and butter.

✪ Add cornstarch to liquid in measuring cup and stir until it dissolves. Pour liquid with cornstarch into saucepan and bring to boil. Reduce heat and cook until sauce thickens slightly.

✪ Remove jalapenos, add cilantro and simmer while steaks cook.

✪ Place steaks on grill for about 3 to 5 minutes and turn to cook other side. Cook about 3 minutes or just until fish is not quite pink in center.

✪ To serve, put each swordfish steak on plate and pour several tablespoons cilantro sauce over top of each. Garnish with grapefruit sections and serve immediately. Serves 8 to 10.

PADRE ISLAND CEVICHE

1 pound red snapper, cut in ½-inch pieces
12 to 15 lemons or 1 (15 ounce) bottle lemon or lime juice
4 to 6 large tomatoes, seeded, chopped
2 large green bell pepper, seeded, minced
4 to 6 green onions with tops, minced
½ cup chopped, seeded mild jalapenos, optional
½ cup oil
1 cup ketchup
Pinch of oregano

✪ Marinate snapper in lemon or lime juice for at least 4 hours. (The action of the lemon or lime juice "cooks" fish and turns snapper to opaque color.)

✪ Add tomatoes, bell peppers, onion, jalapenos, oil, ketchup and oregano. Add jalapenos for desired heat.

✪ Refrigerate several hours or overnight and serve as appetizer. Serves 4.

Stuffed Red Fish

1 (5 pound) red fish, cut into fillets
4 slices white bread
1 cup milk
¼ cup (½ stick) butter
1 small onion, finely minced
1 rib celery, finely chopped
1 (8 ounce) package crabmeat
⅓ cup finely chopped fresh parsley
Dash of cayenne pepper
2 (15 ounce) cans whole tomatoes, drained
2 lemons, sliced
¼ cup (½ stick) butter

✪ Preheat oven to 325°.

✪ In bowl, combine bread with milk. Saute onion and celery in ¼ cup butter and add moistened bread, crab and parsley to make stuffing.

✪ Sprinkle a little salt and pepper and cayenne pepper on fish fillets. Place 1 fillet in large sprayed baking pan and cover with stuffing.

✪ Place another fillet in baking pan and cover with stuffing and repeat process for all fillets.

✪ Place tomatoes and lemon slices around fish fillets. Cut remaining butter into slices and place over fish.

✪ Cover and bake for about 1 hour or until fish flakes easily. Serves 8 to 10.

Dolphin Bay in Corpus Christi is part of the Texas State Aquarium and is a protected environment for Atlantic bottle-nose dolphins that are unable to survive in the wild.

Sea World outside of San Antonio is the largest marine-theme park in the world covering more than 250 acres.

★ROCKPORT SEAFOOD ENCHILADAS

4 green onions with tops, chopped
1 red bell pepper, chopped
4 tomatoes, seeded, chopped
1 clove garlic, minced
2 tablespoons vegetable oil
¾ pound redfish or red snapper, flaked
¾ pound shrimp, peeled, chopped
12 corn tortillas
1 (8 ounce) package shredded Monterey Jack cheese

TOMATILLO SAUCE:
4 green onions with tops, chopped
1 clove garlic, minced
1 tablespoon vegetable oil
3 jalapeno peppers, stemmed, seeded, chopped
10 tomatillos
1 (8 ounce) carton sour cream
1 cup chicken broth
¼ cup snipped cilantro leaves

✪ Preheat oven to 350°.

✪ In skillet saute green onions, bell pepper, tomatoes and garlic in oil until onions are translucent.

✪ Add fish and shrimp, cook until shrimp turns pink and remove from heat. In another skillet or griddle over low heat, soften corn tortillas.

✪ Scoop seafood mixture evenly into center of tortilla and sprinkle cheese on top. Roll tortilla tightly and lay seam side down in sprayed, 10 x 15-inch casserole dish.

TOMATILLO SAUCE:
✪ In skillet saute green onions and garlic in oil until onions are translucent. Place onions and garlic in blender and add all remaining ingredients. Blend until it reaches smooth consistency and pour over enchiladas. Bake for 10 to 15 minutes. Serves 4 to 6.

GULF COAST OYSTER BISQUE

½ cup (1 stick) butter
1 quart oysters, cut up
1 bunch shallots, minced
½ teaspoon minced garlic
3 tablespoons flour
2 pints half-and-half cream
¼ cup dry sherry

✪ In skillet with butter, cook oysters, shallots and garlic until oysters curl. Stir in flour.

✪ In double boiler, heat cream, but do not boil, and add oyster mixture with a little salt and pepper to taste and sherry. Serves 4.

SEASIDE OYSTER LOAF

2 (8 ounce) packages cream cheese, softened
⅔ cup mayonnaise
1 teaspoon hot pepper sauce
2 tablespoons Worcestershire sauce
1 tablespoon milk
2 tablespoons seasoned breadcrumbs
2 (4 ounce) cans smoked oysters, drained, chopped
Parsley for garnish

✪ In mixing bowl, beat cream cheese, mayonnaise, hot pepper sauce, Worcestershire, milk and breadcrumbs. (If mixture is not pliable, add just a little more milk.)

✪ Stir in chopped oysters and place in sprayed 9 x 5-inch loaf pan. Refrigerate about 2 days before serving.

Slim's Tidbit:

"I think tha bravest man in tha world was tha first man to eat an oyster."

 *Editor's Choice*

★LAKE TEXOMA FRIED CATFISH

8 to 10 catfish fillets
1 cup buttermilk
2 cups crushed cracker crumbs or cornmeal
⅓ cup flour
Oil

❂ Dry fish with paper towels and sprinkle with a little salt and pepper.

❂ In bowl, mix cracker crumbs or cornmeal and flour. Dip fillets in buttermilk and in crumb mixture and make sure both sides are well coated.

❂ Heat about ½ inch of oil in skillet and fry fish until light brown and crisp. Serves 4 to 6.

TIP: To make buttermilk, add 1 tablespoon lemon juice or vinegar to 1 cup milk and let it rest for about 10 minutes.

 *Editor's Choice*

★TEXAS FRIED CATFISH

More farm-raised catfish are eaten in Texas than any other state in the U.S.

1½ pounds catfish fillets
Beer
¾ cup cornmeal
½ cup flour
Shortening or oil for frying

❂ Dip fillets in beer, then in mixture of cornmeal, flour, and ½ teaspoon each of salt and pepper and coat well.

❂ Deep fry for 3 to 4 minutes or pan fry at high heat until golden brown. Turn pan-fried fish once. Serves 4.

★KIMBLE COUNTY CABRITO

Mesquite or Spanish oak wood
1 large gunnysack
Wire
1 (10 to 18 pound) suckling goat kid

✪ Dig a dirt pit about 3 feet deep and about 3 feet wide. Build large mesquite or Spanish oak wood fire and burn fire down to make large bed of hot coals.

✪ Wrap skinned, suckling goat kid in foil then in wet gunnysack and tie it with wire.

✪ Place gunnysack on coals, cover with lid of some sort and dirt and cook all day. Serves 14 to 16.

The kitchen-method for preparing cabrito is very simple.

3 to 4 onions, quartered
¾ cup minced garlic
1 cup oil
1 (10 to 18 pound) suckling goat kid, quartered
1 (12 ounce) bottle dark beer
½ cup vegetable oil
1 cup cider vinegar
1 (32 ounce) bottle ketchup
¼ cup prepared yellow mustard
Juice of small lemon
1 cup strong, black coffee
¼ cup chili powder
1 tablespoon Worcestershire sauce

✪ In large roasting pan, cook onions and garlic in oil until they are translucent. Add meat and brown. (Add more oil if necessary.) Sprinkle 1 tablespoon pepper over top and pour beer around meat.

✪ In saucepan mix all remaining ingredients, heat to boiling and pour over meat. Bake at 275° for 2 hours and check liquid. (Add beer if needed.) Bake for another 1 to 2 hours until meat is tender. Serves 14 to 16.

 *Editor's Choice*

★HILL COUNTRY BACKSTRAP

Backstrap is the tenderloin of venison and the very best part.

3 to 4 pound venison backstrap
Milk to cover
1½ cups flour
Oil
Milk or half-and-half cream

✪ Place backstrap in bowl and cover with milk. Soak several hours or overnight in refrigerator.

✪ Remove from milk and cut into ¼-inch slices. In shallow bowl, combine flour, salt and pepper and dredge each backstrap slice in flour mixture.

✪ Fry in oil on medium heat until slices are light brown.

✪ For gravy, use 2 tablespoons seasoned flour and brown in skillet with pan drippings.

✪ Pour in about 2 cups milk or half-and-half cream, stir constantly and cook until gravy thickens. If gravy is too thick, add a little more milk. Serves 6 to 8.

Texas is the largest producer of sheep and lambs in the U.S.

Texas is the largest producer of goats in the U.S.

Texas is the largest producer of wool in the U.S.

Texas is the largest producer of mohair in the U.S.

★CHICKEN-FRIED VENISON STEAK AND PAN GRAVY

2 pounds venison steak, tenderized, thinly sliced
1 cup flour
Oil

PAN GRAVY:
6 to 8 tablespoons pan drippings
6 tablespoons flour
3 cups milk

✪ Season venison with salt and pepper. Dredge all steak pieces in flour mixture until well coated.

✪ Heat about ½ inch oil in heavy skillet and fry steak pieces until golden brown. Remove from skillet and drain on paper towels.

✪ To make gravy, move steaks to warm oven. Add flour to drippings in skillet, stir constantly and cook until flour begins to brown.

✪ Add milk slowly and ½ teaspoon salt and ¼ teaspoon pepper and stir until gravy thickens. Serve in bowl or over steaks. Serves 6 to 8.

TIP: **Bacon drippings make better cream gravy, but it is good just about any way you fix it.**

The white-tail deer is the most important Texas game animal. It is found throughout Texas and is estimated to number in excess of 3,000,000. Exotic deer species have been introduced primarily in central and southern parts of Texas for hunting purposes. The most popular exotic is the axis deer, native to India.

 *Editor's Choice*

MARINATED VENISON ROAST

This is great for appetizers or snacks anytime. It's a terrific recipe for venison.

2 to 3 pounds venison roast, cooked
3 onions, sliced in rings
8 to 10 fresh mushrooms, halved
2 (3 ounce) jars capers, drained
¼ cup red wine vinegar
¾ cup oil
1 teaspoon sugar

✪ Cut venison into bite-size pieces.

✪ In large bowl, layer venison, onions, mushrooms and capers.

✪ In separate bowl, mix vinegar, oil, sugar, ½ teaspoon salt and ½ teaspoon black pepper and mix well. Pour over venison and mix additional cups of red wine vinegar, oil, sugar, salt and black pepper as needed to cover venison.

✪ Cover and marinate at least 1 to 2 days before serving. Stir occasionally. Serves 6 to 8.

TIP: Cooking Venison Roast
The best way to cook a roast or ham for this recipe is to season it liberally with salt and pepper. Place in roasting pan and add 1 to 2 cups water. Bake roast at 300° for about 3 to 4 hours or until fork-tender. Check to make sure there is enough water and venison does not dry out.

⟣⟶ *Slim's Tidbit:* ⟵⟢

"Buck fever's a severe disease that affects hunters' eyesight and hand-eye coordination. Some hunters say they can't tell the diff'rence between horns and branches."

SLOW-COOKIN' VENISON ROAST

MARINADE:
1 cup ketchup
1 cup chili sauce
4 cloves garlic, minced
1 onion, minced
1 jalapeno, seeded, chopped
¼ cup packed brown sugar
3 tablespoons liquid smoke
¼ cup vinegar
¼ cup Worcestershire sauce
2 teaspoons dry mustard

ROAST:
2 to 3 pounds venison roast
2 teaspoons chili powder

✪ In large bowl mix all marinade ingredients. Whisk several minutes to mix well.

✪ Place roast in large slow cooker and season with 1 teaspoon salt, 1 teaspoon pepper and chili powder. Pour marinade over roast.

✪ Turn sprayed slow cooker to LOW, cover and cook 6 to 8 hours or until roast is tender. Serves 8.

The armadillo is the official small mammal of the State of Texas. The nine-banded armadillo is found throughout most of Texas.

★REAL TEXAS VENISON CHILI

Beef suet or 2 to 4 tablespoons vegetable oil
3 pounds venison, cubed
1 pound ground pork sausage
3 to 6 dried, chile colorado peppers, ground, seeded
1 to 2 whole jalapeno peppers, divided
4 cloves garlic, minced
1 tablespoon ground cumin
1 tablespoon oregano
2 tablespoons masa harina

✪ Cook suet in large skillet until fat separates from connective tissue or
use vegetable oil for healthier cooking. Brown venison on all sides.
Brown pork sausage and drain.

✪ Pour venison and sausage and oil in large kettle or roasting pan with
ground chile peppers, 1 whole jalapeno and enough water to be about
2 inches above venison.

✪ Bring water to boil, reduce heat and simmer about 2 to 3 hours. Stir
occasionally and skim off grease.

✪ Add garlic, cumin, oregano and 1 tablespoon salt, cover and simmer
another 1 hour. Stir occasionally and skim off grease.

✪ Check seasonings and add whole jalapeno if not hot enough. Add
masa harina if chili is too thin and simmer another 30 minutes to
1 hour. Serves 8 to 10.

TIP: Masa harina is flour made from masa which is sun-dried or oven-dried
corn kernels used to make corn tortillas.

RANCH-VENISON CHILI
Chase this "bowl of red" with flour tortillas and jalapenos.

¼ cup olive oil
4 onions, minced
2 to 3 pounds venison, cubed
1 pound ground pork sausage or bacon, optional
6 to 8 dried New Mexico Red chile peppers, ground
3 to 4 jalapenos, seeded, chopped
2 to 3 cloves garlic, minced
2 teaspoons paprika
2 teaspoons cumin

✪ In large Dutch oven or heavy roasting pan, brown onions in oil until they are translucent.

✪ Add cubed venison, a little at a time, and brown on all sides. Sprinkle salt and pepper on venison as it browns. Add a little oil if needed.

✪ Pour in 1 to 2 cups water, New Mexico Reds, jalapenos, garlic, paprika and cumin and stir well.

✪ Cook over high heat, uncovered, for about 10 minutes, then reduce heat to low and cook 2 to 3 hours. (Add 1 to 2 cups more water if needed for consistency desired. Adjust seasonings if water is added.)

✪ Reduce heat to simmer and cook another 1 to 2 hours. Serves 8 to 10.

TIP: **Dried New Mexico Red chile peppers are great in chili. They are sweet to mild. They are found in ristras in New Mexico and in Texas border towns.**

DEER CAMP STEW

1 (28 ounce) can Mexican stewed tomatoes
2 (15 ounce) cans beef broth
2 to 3 pounds venison, cubed
Bacon drippings or olive oil
1 (6 ounce) bottle Worcestershire sauce
2 to 3 teaspoons paprika
2 to 3 jalapenos, seeded, chopped
5 to 6 potatoes, chopped
3 to 4 large onions, chopped
1 (16 ounce) bag baby carrots, sliced
3 to 4 ribs celery, chopped

✪ Pour tomatoes and beef broth into large Dutch oven or large stew pot and turn heat to warm.

✪ In large skillet brown venison in bacon drippings. Pour venison and pan drippings into stew pot.

✪ Add Worcestershire sauce, paprika, 2 teaspoons salt, 2 teaspoons pepper and jalapenos. Bring stew to boil, reduce heat to low and cook about 2 to 3 hours or until venison is fairly tender.

✪ Add potatoes, onions and carrots and cook on low heat another 1 to 2 hours. Adjust seasonings to taste as stew cooks.

✪ Add celery about 15 to 20 minutes before serving to give stew a little crunch. Serves 8 to 10.

―――◆―――

Slim's Tidbit:

"You know good chili is a work in process. You gotta study tha thang to git it right an' you gotta stay with it. Add your own two cents worth to a chili recipe so ya can lay claim to it."

VENISON JERKY

2 tablespoons vinegar
2 tablespoons steak sauce
1 teaspoon liquid smoke
1 teaspoon garlic salt
1 to 3 jalapenos, seeded, chopped
1 onion, minced
2 to 3 pounds venison

✪ In large bowl, mix vinegar, steak sauce, liquid smoke, garlic salt and ½ teaspoon pepper and whisk thoroughly. Add jalapenos and onion to marinade and set aside.

✪ Cut venison into strips about ¼ inch thick and about 1 inch wide.

✪ Add venison to marinade and mix well. Make sure all venison is covered with marinade. Seal and store in refrigerator for 24 hours.

✪ Remove from refrigerator, drain venison strips and place on baking sheet with space in between all pieces.

✪ Bake at 200° for about 3 to 5 hours. Turn once or twice while cooking. Serves 8 to 12.

The bobcat is found in large numbers in all areas of Texas. The cougar and puma are found primarily in the mountainous regions and along the Rio Grande brushland.

★GRILLED DOVE AND MEXICAN BULLETS

MARINADE:
¾ cup tarragon vinegar
¼ cup Worcestershire sauce
¼ cup sugar
2 teaspoons garlic powder
1 teaspoon seasoned salt
¼ teaspoon ground coriander
1 cup oil

8 to 10 doves, cleaned
5 to 6 jalapenos, seeded, halved
1 (1 pound) package Colby cheese
8 to 10 slices bacon

✪ In large glass bowl or baking dish, mix all marinade ingredients and set aside.

✪ Slice breasts off doves and drop in marinade. Cover bowl, refrigerate and marinate at least 24 hours. Stir marinade and dove several times to blend ingredients.

✪ Remove dove breasts from marinade and discard marinade.

✪ Drain breasts and make a sandwich using one breast, one jalapeno half, one slice cheese and one breast together. Tie together with one slice bacon and secure with toothpick.

✪ Place on grill over medium fire and cook until bacon is crispy. Turn several times while grilling. Serves 4.

⟫◆⟪

Slim's Tidbit:
If ya cain't figur' it out, Meskun bullets are "hal a pain yos".

★FRIED DOVE AND GRAVY

2 eggs, beaten
⅓ cup milk
1 to 1½ cups flour
½ teaspoon seasoned salt
¼ teaspoon curry powder
10 to 12 doves
Oil
1 to 2 cups milk

✪ In shallow bowl, combine eggs and ⅓ cup milk.

✪ In another shallow bowl, combine flour, seasoned salt, ½ teaspoon pepper and curry powder.

✪ Dredge each dove in seasoned flour, dip in egg-milk mixture and again in flour mixture.

✪ Brown doves slowly in skillet with a little oil. Drain doves on paper towels.

✪ To make gravy, do not wash skillet and add 2 tablespoons of remaining seasoned flour.

✪ On medium heat, brown flour until golden brown and add milk, stirring constantly until gravy thickens. Serve over mashed potatoes or biscuits or both. Serves 4 to 5.

There are more than 540 species of birds in Texas, more than three-fourths of all bird species found in the United States.

BAKED QUAIL

2 tablespoons (¼ stick) butter
2 bunches fresh green onions with tops, chopped
⅔ cup flour
8 quail
1 (10 ounce) can cream of chicken soup
½ cup cream sherry

✪ Preheat oven to 225°. In skillet, saute onions and remove to plate. Combine a little salt and pepper and flour and dip quail in flour mixture, coating well.

✪ Brown quail in skillet with remaining butter. Transfer quail to shallow baking dish.

✪ Return onion to skillet, add soup and sherry and mix while cooking on medium heat.

✪ Pour mixture over quail, cover tightly and bake for 2 hours. Serves 4 to 5.

FRIED GAME BIRDS

10 to 12 quail or dove
1 (6 ounce) can frozen orange juice concentrate, thawed
1 teaspoon lemon juice
1 to 2 cups biscuit mix
Oil

✪ In large shallow bowl, combine orange juice concentrate, lemon juice and ½ teaspoon salt. Place birds in bowl, add enough water to cover birds and marinate for 2 to 3 hours. Discard marinade.

✪ Pour biscuit mix in shallow bowl and dredge birds in biscuit mix to cover well.

✪ Fry birds in heated, deep-fat fryer until light brown. Drain on paper towels and serve hot. Serves 5 to 6.

QUAIL IN CREAM SAUCE

6 to 8 quail
Flour
3 tablespoons butter
½ cup finely chopped fresh mushrooms
½ cup chopped fresh green onions
1 tablespoon chopped fresh parsley
⅔ cup white wine
⅔ cup whipping cream
Cooked rice

✪ Preheat oven to 325°.

✪ Sprinkle quail with salt and pepper, roll in flour, and coat well. In skillet melt butter and lightly brown quail. Transfer to sprayed baking dish.

✪ Saute mushrooms and onions in same skillet and add a little more butter, if necessary. Add parsley and white wine and pour over quail.

✪ Bake covered for 45 to 50 minutes, basting twice.

✪ Add whipping cream and cook additional 10 minutes. Serve over hot cooked rice. Serves 4.

TIP: Use this recipe for cooking dove as well.

Because Texas is on the migratory path between North, Central and South America for many species of birds, it has become a world-class bird-watching destination. The World Birding Center in the Lower Rio Grande Valley protects wildlife habitat and offers educational centers and observation sites for more than 450 species of birds.

The World's Largest Rattlesnake Round-Up is held in Sweetwater in March and hosts brisket and chili cook-offs.

WILD TURKEY BREASTS

This is a real delicacy and hunters really look forward to this meal.

Dressed wild turkey breasts
Freshly ground black pepper
Flour
Milk
Cooking oil

✪ Slice turkey breasts in thin strips across the grain.

✪ Season generously with salt and pepper. Dip both sides in flour, dip in milk and again in flour.

✪ Place in large, heavy skillet with hot oil and cook on both sides until golden brown. Do not overcook. Drain on paper towels and serve immediately.

FRIED RATTLESNAKE

Rattlesnake, cleaned, skinned
Freshly ground black pepper
Cornmeal
Buttermilk
Oil

✪ Slice rattlesnake in medallions about ½ to ¾ inch thick.

✪ Season generously with salt and pepper. Dip both sides in cornmeal, dip in buttermilk and again in cornmeal.

✪ Place in large, heavy skillet with hot oil and cook on both sides until golden brown. Do not overcook. Drain on paper towels and serve immediately.

TIP: **To make buttermilk, mix 1 cup milk with 1 tablespoon lemon juice or vinegar and let milk rest for about 10 minutes.**

Editor's Choice

PAN-FRIED FROG LEGS

If you are ever lucky enough to run into some frog legs, be sure to cook 'em just like this.

10 pair frog legs
2 eggs, beaten
2 tablespoons milk
Flour
Oil or shortening

GRAVY, OPTIONAL:
3 tablespoons flour
1 to 1½ cups milk

✪ Salt and pepper each set of frog legs.

✪ Add milk to beaten eggs and dip frog legs into egg mixture. Roll in flour and coat frog legs well.

✪ Heat about ¼ inch oil or shortening in heavy skillet and brown frog legs on both sides. Lower heat and cook until tender, about 15 to 20 minutes.

✪ To make gravy, remove frog legs from skillet and add 3 tablespoons flour, ½ teaspoon salt and ½ teaspoon pepper. Turn burner to high heat and add milk, stirring constantly, until gravy thickens. Serves 4 to 6.

⤐ *Slim's Tidbit:* ⤐
"I really like 'ese thangs. I call 'em pond chickens."

Austin, Texas has the largest urban bat population in North America estimated at more than 1,500,000 that live under the Congress Avenue Bridge.

KILLER PIECE-OF-TAIL CHILI

This won first place in the Cedar Mills Yacht Club Chili Cook-Off. The alligator meat came from the section of the tail behind the back feet, hence "a piece of tail". A cookbook committee member in Louisiana came through with the fresh alligator meat.

3 to 3½ pounds alligator meat
½ to 1 pound suet
7 tablespoons ground peppercorns, divided
¼ cup hot sauce, divided
3 large yellow onions, diced
3 large bell peppers, seeded, diced
3 to 5 cloves garlic, chopped
1 cup oil
5 large tomatoes, diced
3 (6 ounce) cans tomato paste
12 to 15 dried New Mexico Red chiles, ground
3 tablespoons cumin
½ to 1 cup diced jalapenos
1½ to 2 cups red wine

✪ Dice alligator meat and suet and boil in 4 to 5 cups water for about 20 to 30 minutes with 3 tablespoons salt, 3 tablespoons ground peppercorns and 2 tablespoons hot sauce.

✪ Saute onions, bell pepper, garlic and 2 tablespoons ground peppercorns in oil.

✪ Reduce alligator meat to simmer and stir in onion, bell pepper, garlic and peppercorns.

✪ Add tomatoes and tomato paste and mix thoroughly.

✪ Add ground chiles, 2 tablespoons hot sauce, 1 tablespoon salt, 2 tablespoons peppercorns, cumin and simmer 5 to 10 minutes.

✪ Add jalapenos to taste. Stir in red wine and simmer for 2 to 4 hours to blend flavors and tenderize meat. Serve hot. Serves 10.

TIP: Coat fingers with oil to cut the sting of the jalapenos or wear rubber gloves.

HOT, BAKED ARMADILLO EGGS

10 jalapenos
1 (12 ounce) package shredded cheddar cheese
1 (1 pound) package ground pork sausage
1 (10 count) refrigerated biscuits

✪ Preheat oven to 325°.

✪ Cut down on side of jalapeno and remove seeds and stems. Rinse and dry well with paper towels. Stuff jalapenos with cheese.

✪ Slice sausage and flatten with hand to about ¼ inch thick. Wrap around jalapeno and put in sprayed baking dish.

✪ Bake for about 20 minutes or until sausage browns. Turn once while cooking. Remove from oven and drain on paper towels.

✪ Wrap biscuit dough around each "egg" and seal the edges. Bake until each biscuit is golden brown. (Just kidding 'bout those armadillos.) Serves 6 to 8.

WILD COOK-OFFS

The Celebrity Quail Hunt is held in Abilene in February.

The Wild Hog Festival is held in Sabinal in February.

The LaSalle County Fair and Wild Hog Cook-Off is held in Cotulla in February.

The Annual Electra Goat Barbecue is held in Electra in May.

The Texas Gatorfest is held in Anahuac in September.

The One-Arm Dove Hunt is held in Olney in September.

The World Championship Barbecue Goat Cook-Off is held in Brady in September.

The World Championship Wild Hog Barbecue Cook-Off is held in Crowell in November.

Yes siree bob!

Sweet Cakes
Pies & Cobblers
Momma's Cookies
Squares & Bars
Sweet Thangs

Official Tree of The State of Texas

PECAN

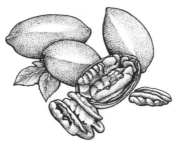

Slim's Tidbit:

"Can't beat it with a stick."

THE BEST FRESH APPLE CAKE

1½ cups oil
2 cups sugar
3 eggs
2½ cups sifted flour
½ teaspoon baking soda
2 teaspoons baking powder
½ teaspoon ground cinnamon
1 teaspoon vanilla
3 cups peeled, grated apples
1 cup chopped pecans

GLAZE:
2 tablespoons butter, melted
2 tablespoons milk
1 cup powdered sugar
1 teaspoon vanilla
¼ teaspoon lemon extract

✪ Preheat oven to 350°. Spray and flour tube pan.

✪ Mix oil, sugar and eggs and beat well.

✪ In separate bowl, combine flour, ½ teaspoon salt, baking soda, baking powder and cinnamon. Gradually add flour mixture to creamed mixture.

✪ Add vanilla, fold in apples and pecans and pour into tube pan.

✪ Bake for 1 hour. While cake is still warm, invert onto serving plate.

GLAZE:

✪ Combine and mix all ingredients and drizzle over cake while cake is still warm. Serves 18 to 20.

RICH TURTLE CAKE

1 (18 ounce) box German chocolate cake mix
½ cup (1 stick) butter, softened
½ cup oil
1 (14 ounce) can sweetened condensed milk, divided
1 cup chopped pecans
1 (16 ounce) bag caramels, wrappers removed

FROSTING:
½ cup (1 stick) butter
¼ cup cocoa
4 to 5 tablespoons milk
1 (16 ounce) box powdered sugar
1 teaspoon vanilla

✪ Preheat oven to 350°.

✪ In mixing bowl, combine cake mix, butter, 1½ cups water, oil and half can sweetened, condensed milk and beat well.

✪ Fold in pecans and pour half batter into sprayed, floured 9 x 13-inch baking dish. Bake for 25 minutes.

✪ In saucepan, combine caramels and remaining condensed milk, spread evenly over baked cake and cover with remaining batter. Bake for additional 20 to 25 minutes.

FROSTING:

✪ In saucepan, melt butter, add cocoa and milk and mix well.

✪ Add powdered sugar and vanilla and stir well. (If frosting seems too stiff, add 1 tablespoon milk.) Spread over warm, but not hot, cake. Serves 12 to 14.

PINA COLADA CAKE

1 (18 ounce) box pineapple cake mix
3 eggs
⅓ cup oil
1 (14 ounce) can sweetened condensed milk
1 (15 ounce) can cream of coconut
1 cup flaked coconut
1 (8 ounce) can crushed pineapple, drained
1 (8 ounce) carton whipped topping

✪ Preheat oven to 350°.

✪ In mixing bowl, combine cake mix, eggs, 1¼ cups water and oil. Beat 3 to 4 minutes and pour into sprayed, floured 10 x 15-inch baking pan. Bake for 35 minutes.

✪ When cake is done, punch holes in top with fork so frosting will soak into cake.

✪ Mix sweetened condensed milk, coconut cream, coconut and pineapple.

✪ While cake is still warm, pour mixture over top of cake. Refrigerate about 1 hour, spread whipped topping over cake and return to refrigerator. Serves 12 to 14.

The McDonald Observatory, northwest of Fort Davis, is one of the best astronomical research facilities in the world.

★Mockingbird Cake

3 cups flour
2 cups sugar
1 teaspoon baking soda
1 teaspoon ground cinnamon
3 eggs, beaten
1½ cups oil
1½ teaspoons vanilla
1 (8-ounce) can crushed pineapple with juice
1 cup chopped pecans
½ cup flaked coconut
2 bananas, mashed

GLAZE:
1 cup sugar
½ cup buttermilk
1 tablespoon corn syrup
¼ teaspoon baking soda
1 teaspoon vanilla
1 tablespoon butter

✪ Preheat oven to 325°.

✪ In large mixing bowl, combine flour, sugar, baking soda, ½ teaspoon salt and cinnamon, and stir well. Add eggs, oil and vanilla and stir only until dry ingredients are moist, but do not beat.

✪ Stir in pineapple, pecans, coconut and bananas. Spoon batter into sprayed, floured tube pan and bake for 1 hour 15 minutes. Test with toothpick for doneness. Remove pan when slightly cool.

GLAZE:

✪ Bring all ingredients and ¼ teaspoon salt to boil and stir constantly. Remove from heat, cool for 4 to 5 minutes and pour over cake slowly.

✪ Punch holes in cake with toothpicks so glaze will soak into cake. Serves 18 to 20.

CHOCOLATE ROUND-UP CAKE

2 cups sugar
2 cups flour
½ cup (1 stick) butter
½ cup oil
4 heaping tablespoons cocoa
½ cup buttermilk
2 eggs, beaten
1 teaspoon baking soda
1 teaspoon ground cinnamon
1 teaspoon vanilla

FROSTING:
½ cup (1 stick) butter, melted
¼ cup cocoa
6 tablespoons milk
1 (1 pound) box powdered sugar
1 teaspoon vanilla
1 cup chopped pecans
1 (10 ounce) can flaked coconut

✪ Preheat oven to 350°.

✪ Blend sugar and flour in mixing bowl and set aside.

✪ In saucepan, bring butter, oil, cocoa and 1 cup water to boil, pour over flour and sugar mixture and beat well. Add buttermilk, eggs, baking soda, cinnamon, vanilla and ½ teaspoon salt.

✪ Mix well and pour in sprayed, floured 9 x 13-inch pan and bake for 40 to 45 minutes.

FROSTING:

✪ Five minutes before cake is done, combine butter, cocoa, milk, powdered sugar and vanilla and mix well.

✪ Add pecans and coconut, mix well and spread on hot cake. Serves 12.

PUMPKIN-CHESS CAKE

1 (18 ounce) box yellow cake mix
¾ cup (1½ sticks) butter, softened, divided
4 eggs, divided
1 (15 ounce) can pumpkin
2 teaspoons ground cinnamon
½ cup packed brown sugar
⅔ cup milk
½ cup sugar
⅔ cup chopped pecans

✪ Preheat oven to 350°.

✪ Set aside 1 cup cake mix. Mix rest of cake mix, ½ cup butter and 1 egg and press into sprayed 9 x 13-inch pan.

✪ Mix pumpkin, 3 eggs, cinnamon, brown sugar and milk and pour over batter in pan.

✪ Use remaining cake mix, sugar, remaining butter and chopped pecans to make topping and crumble over cake. Bake for 1 hour. Serves 12 to 14.

CHOCOLATE-ORANGE CAKE

1 (16 ounce) loaf frozen pound cake, thawed
1 (12 ounce) jar orange marmalade
1 (16 ounce) can ready-to-spread chocolate fudge frosting

✪ Cut cake horizontally into 3 layers. Place one layer on cake platter and spread with one-half of marmalade. Place second layer over first and spread on remaining marmalade. Top with third cake layer and spread frosting liberally on top and sides of cake. Refrigerate before serving. Serves 8.

PUMPKIN-PIE POUND CAKE

1 cup shortening
1¼ cups sugar
¾ cup packed brown sugar
5 eggs, room temperature
1 cup canned pumpkin
2½ cups flour
2 teaspoons ground cinnamon
1 teaspoon ground nutmeg
1 teaspoon baking soda
½ cup orange juice, room temperature
2 teaspoons vanilla
1½ cups chopped pecans

FROSTING:
1 (16 ounce) box powdered sugar
6 tablespoons (¾ stick) butter, melted
2 to 3 tablespoons orange juice
¼ teaspoon orange extract

✪ In mixing bowl, cream shortening and both sugars for about 4 minutes. Add eggs, one at a time, and mix well after each addition. Blend in pumpkin.

✪ In separate bowl, mix flour, spices, ¼ teaspoon salt and baking soda and mix well.

✪ Gradually beat dry ingredients into batter until ingredients mix well.

✪ Fold in orange juice, vanilla and chopped pecans. Pour into sprayed, floured bundt pan.

✪ Bake for 70 to 75 minutes or until tester comes out clean.

✪ Allow cake to rest in pan for about 15 minutes. Turn cake out onto rack to cool completely before frosting.

✪ For frosting, thoroughly mix all frosting ingredients using only 2 tablespoons orange juice. Add more orange juice if icing seems too stiff. Serves 18.

 *Editor's Choice*

MOM'S POUND CAKE

This is an old-fashion pound cake that cannot be beaten.

1 cup (2 sticks) butter
2 cups sugar
5 eggs
1 teaspoon vanilla
2 cups flour
1 cup chopped pecans

✪ Preheat oven to 350°.

✪ In large bowl cream butter, sugar, eggs and vanilla.

✪ In separate bowl, mix flour and ½ teaspoon salt. Slowly mix flour mixture with sugar mixture.

✪ Pour evenly into sprayed, floured bundt pan. Sprinkle chopped pecans on top.

✪ Bake for about 40 minutes. Insert toothpick in center. It is done when toothpick comes out clean. Serves 18.

Kids learn how to spell Dallas, by reciting the phrase, "Big D, little a, double -- l, a – s."

 *Editor's Choice*

NUTTY POUND CAKE

1 cup (2 sticks) butter, softened
2 cups sugar
5 large eggs
1 teaspoon vanilla
1 teaspoon butter flavoring
1 teaspoon almond extract
2 cups flour, divided
2 cups chopped pecans

✪ Preheat oven to 325°.

✪ In mixing bowl, cream butter and sugar and beat in eggs, one at a time.

✪ Stir in vanilla, butter and almond flavorings. Add 1¾ cups flour and beat well.

✪ Combine remaining flour with pecans and fold into batter.

✪ Bake in sprayed, floured bundt pan for 70 to 75 minutes.

✪ Cool, remove cake from pan and dust with powdered sugar. Serves 18.

The Nasher Sculpture Center in the arts district of Dallas is considered to be the finest private collection in the world. Sculptures are both indoors and outdoors and fill the 2½-acre site.

A Really Great Pound Cake

½ cup shortening
1 cup butter
3 cups sugar
5 eggs
3½ cups flour
½ teaspoon baking powder
1 cup milk
1 teaspoon rum flavoring
1 teaspoon coconut flavoring

GLAZE:
⅓ cup sugar
½ teaspoon almond extract

✪ Preheat oven to 325°.

✪ Cream shortening, butter and sugar. Add eggs and beat well.

✪ Mix flour and baking powder. Add dry ingredients and milk alternately to butter mixture, beginning and ending with flour.

✪ Add rum and coconut flavorings. Pour into large sprayed, floured tube pan.

✪ Bake for 1 hour 30 minutes to 1 hour 45 minutes. (Do not open door during baking.) Test with toothpick for doneness.

GLAZE:

✪ Right before cake is done, bring 1 cup water and sugar to rolling boil. Remove from heat and add almond extract.

✪ While cake is still in pan and right out of the oven, pour glaze over cake and let stand about 30 minutes before removing from pan. Serves 18.

BROWN SUGAR-RUM CAKE

1½ cups (3 sticks) butter, softened
1 (15 ounce) box light brown sugar
1 cup sugar
5 large eggs
¼ cup milk
¼ cup rum
2 teaspoons vanilla
3 cups flour
2 teaspoons baking powder
1½ cups chopped pecans

✪ Preheat oven to 325°.

✪ With electric mixer, beat butter and sugars for about 5 minutes. Add eggs, one at a time, and beat just until yellow disappears.

✪ In separate bowl, combine milk, rum and vanilla. In separate bowl, combine flour, baking powder and ¼ teaspoon salt.

✪ Add half flour mixture to butter mixture and beat at low speed. Add milk mixture and mix.

✪ Add remaining flour mixture, beat at low speed and fold in pecans.

✪ Pour into sprayed, floured tube pan. Bake for 1 hour 20 minutes. Test with toothpick to make sure cake is done.

✪ Cool in pan for 20 minutes. Remove from pan, sprinkle with powdered sugar, if desired, and continue to cool. Serves 18 to 20.

The Kimbell Art Museum in Fort Worth is considered to be the finest small museum in the world and to be the greatest museum building in the late 20th century.

SOUTH TEXAS TROPICAL CHEESECAKE

1¼ cups graham cracker crumbs
½ cup flaked coconut
½ cup chopped pecans
2 tablespoons light brown sugar
¼ cup (½ stick) butter, melted
2 (8 ounce) packages cream cheese, softened
1 (14 ounce) can sweetened condensed milk
3 eggs
¼ cup frozen orange juice concentrate, thawed
1 teaspoon pineapple extract
1 (20 ounce) can pineapple pie filling, divided
1 cup sour cream

✪ Preheat oven to 300°.

✪ Combine crumbs, coconut, pecans, brown sugar and butter. Press firmly into sprayed 9-inch springform pan and set aside.

✪ In large mixing bowl, beat cream cheese until fluffy. Gradually beat in condensed milk.

✪ Add eggs, juice concentrate and pineapple extract and mix well. Stir in ¾ cup pineapple pie filling.

✪ Pour into sprayed springform pan. Bake for 1 hour or until center is set.

✪ Spread top with sour cream and bake for 5 minutes longer. Cool, spread remaining pineapple pie filling over cheesecake and refrigerate. Serves 12 to 16.

When it was built, the Astrodome in Houston was the first domed sports stadium in the world.

VERY BLUEBERRY CHEESECAKE

34 vanilla wafers, crushed
6 tablespoons (¾ stick) butter, melted
1 (.25 ounce) envelope unflavored gelatin
2 (8 ounce) packages cream cheese, softened
1 tablespoon lemon juice
1 (7 ounce) jar marshmallow creme
¼ cup powdered sugar
1 (16 ounce) can blueberries, drained
1 (8 ounce) carton whipped topping

✪ Place crumbs in sprayed 9-inch springform pan. Pour melted butter in pan, mix well and pat down.

✪ In saucepan, soften gelatin in ¼ cup cold water. Place over low heat just until it dissolves.

✪ Combine cream cheese, lemon juice, marshmallow creme, powdered sugar and gelatin and beat until smooth.

✪ Puree blueberries in blender. Fold whipped topping and pureed blueberries into cream cheese mixture and pour into springform pan. Refrigerate several hours before serving. Serves 12 to 14.

The giraffe standing at the entrance of the Dallas Zoo is 7 inches taller than the 66-foot tall statue of Sam Houston along Interstate 45 just south of Huntsville. It is the tallest statue in Texas.

WHITE CHOCOLATE PIE

4 ounces white chocolate
20 large marshmallows
½ cup milk
1 (8 ounce) carton whipped topping
½ cup chopped pecans
½ cup maraschino cherries, chopped, well drained
1 (9-inch) piecrust, baked

✪ In double boiler, melt white chocolate, marshmallows and milk and cool.

✪ Add whipped topping, pecans and cherries, pour in piecrust and freeze.

✪ Remove from freezer 5 to 10 minutes before serving. Serves 8.

FLUFFY PECAN PIE

3 large egg whites
1 teaspoon cream of tartar
1 cup sugar
12 soda crackers, crushed
1½ teaspoons vanilla
1½ cups chopped pecans

✪ Preheat oven to 350°.

✪ Beat egg whites with cream of tartar until frothy. Gradually add sugar and continue beating until stiff peaks form.

✪ Fold in crackers, vanilla and pecans mix well.

✪ Pour into 9-inch glass pie pan. Bake for about 30 minutes or until pie is firm. Serves 8.

 *Editor's Choice*

★TEXAS PECAN PIE

1 cup pecan halves
1 (9-inch) piecrust
1 cup corn syrup
¾ cup sugar
3 tablespoons butter, melted
1 teaspoon vanilla
3 eggs, slightly beaten

✪ Preheat oven to 375°.

✪ Place pecans in piecrust and make sure pecans are evenly distributed in crust.

✪ In bowl, combine corn syrup, sugar, butter, vanilla and eggs and mix well. Pour into piecrust and rearrange pecans, if necessary.

✪ Place 1-inch strips of foil around edges of piecrust to keep crust from browning too much.

✪ Bake for 10 minutes, reduce heat to 325° and bake for 45 minutes or until center sets. Serves 8.

PINK LEMONADE PIE

1 (6 ounce) can frozen pink lemonade concentrate, thawed
1 (14 ounce) can sweetened condensed milk
1 (12 ounce) carton whipped topping
1 (9 inch) graham cracker pie crust

✪ In large bowl, combine lemonade concentrate and condensed milk and mix well. Fold in whipped topping and pour into pie crust. Refrigerate several hours. Serves 8.

 *Editor's Choice*

★Margarita Pie

1 (14 ounce) can sweetened condensed milk
2 eggs, separated
¾ cup sugar, divided
⅓ cup fresh lime juice
¼ cup tequila
¼ cup triple sec liqueur
1 (9 inch) graham cracker crust
1 (8 ounce) carton whipping cream
Lime slices for garnish

✪ Preheat oven to 325°.

✪ In mixing bowl, combine sweetened condensed milk, egg yolks, ½ cup sugar, lime juice, tequila and triple sec and mix well.

✪ Beat egg whites until slightly stiff and fold into egg-sugar mixture.

✪ Spoon mixture into piecrust, bake for 25 minutes or until set and cool.

✪ Beat whipping cream, add ¼ cup sugar and spread over cooled pie.

✪ Refrigerate several hours or overnight. When ready to serve, slice lime very thin and make cut to center of each lime slice, twist and place on each serving for garnish. Serves 8.

 *Editor's Choice*

★PUMPKIN-CHIFFON PIE

This pie is fabulous and it makes regular pumpkin pie seem ordinary.

1 (.25 ounce) envelope unflavored gelatin
2 eggs
1¼ cups sugar
1¼ cups canned pumpkin
⅔ cup milk
½ teaspoon ground ginger
½ teaspoon ground nutmeg
½ teaspoon ground cinnamon
1 (8 ounce) carton whipping cream
1 (9 inch) piecrust, baked

✪ Soften gelatin in ¼ cup cold water and set aside.

✪ With mixer, beat eggs about 3 minutes. Add sugar, pumpkin, milk, spices and ½ teaspoon salt and mix well. Pour mixture into double boiler over medium heat, stir continuously and cook until it reaches custard consistency.

✪ Mix in softened gelatin and dissolve in hot pumpkin mixture.

✪ After mixture cools, whip cream until very stiff and fold into pumpkin mixture. (Do not use frozen, whipped topping.)

✪ Pour into baked piecrust and refrigerate several hours before slicing. Serves 8.

PARTY PUMPKIN PIE

1 (15 ounce) can pumpkin
1 cup sugar
3 eggs, slightly beaten
½ teaspoon ground cinnamon
¼ teaspoon ground ginger
¼ teaspoon ground nutmeg
¼ teaspoon ground allspice
1½ cups half-and-half cream
2 tablespoons bourbon
½ cup flaked coconut
1 (10 inch) piecrust

✪ Preheat oven to 350°.

✪ In bowl, combine pumpkin, sugar and eggs and beat well.

✪ Add spices, ⅛ teaspoon salt, cream, bourbon and coconut and mix well.

✪ Pour into piecrust and bake for 35 to 40 minutes or until center is set. Serves 8.

The largest medical complex in the world is Texas Medical Center in Houston, Texas. It includes 2 medical schools, 4 nursing schools, 14 hospitals, 55,000 employees, almost 7,000 patient beds, 37,000 parking spaces, 100 buildings with 20,000,000 square feet and 12 miles of streets on 675 acres.

OLD-TIME PINEAPPLE-CHESS PIE

1½ cups sugar
1 tablespoon cornmeal
2 tablespoons flour
6 tablespoons (¾ stick) butter, melted
2 eggs, beaten
1 (8 ounce) can crushed pineapple with juice
1 (9 inch) piecrust

✪ Preheat oven to 350°.

✪ Combine sugar, cornmeal, flour and pinch of salt and mix. Stir in butter, eggs and pineapple and beat.

✪ Pour into piecrust and bake for 45 minutes. Serves 8.

———⊱◆⊰———

The world's biggest oil gusher was Spindletop near Beaumont in 1901. The gusher blew more than 100 feet in the air and spewed more than 100,000 gallons of oil per day for 9 days before it was capped.

The largest known mammal colony in the world is the colony of 20,000,000 or more Mexican freetail bats in Bracken Bat Cave, located in Comal County. The largest urban colony resides under the Congress Street Bridge in Austin.

CREAMY LEMON PIE

1 (8 ounce) package cream cheese, softened
1 (14 ounce) can sweetened condensed milk
¼ cup lemon juice
1 (20 ounce) can lemon pie filling
1 (9 inch) graham cracker piecrust

✪ In mixing bowl, cream cheese until smooth. Add sweetened condensed milk and lemon juice and beat until mixture is very creamy.

✪ Fold in lemon pie filling and stir well. Pour into piecrust. Refrigerate several hours before slicing and serving. Serves 8.

★LEMON-CHESS PIE

1¼ cups sugar
3 large eggs
½ cup corn syrup
1 tablespoon cornmeal
¾ cup sour cream
½ teaspoon vanilla
¼ cup lemon juice
1 (8 inch) piecrust

✪ Preheat oven to 350°.

✪ In bowl, beat sugar and eggs and mix well. Fold in corn syrup, cornmeal, sour cream, vanilla and lemon juice and mix well. Pour into piecrust.

✪ Cut 1½-inch strips of foil and cover edges of crust to keep crust from getting too brown.

✪ Bake for 45 to 50 minutes or until knife placed in center of pie comes out clean. Serves 8.

Lemon Meringue Pie

1½ cups sugar
⅓ cup flour
4 large egg yolks, beaten
⅓ cup lemon juice

MERINGUE:
4 large egg whites
¼ teaspoon cream of tartar
¼ cup sugar
1 (9 inch) piecrust, baked

✪ Preheat oven to 350°.

✪ Combine sugar, flour, egg yolks, lemon juice and pinch of salt in double boiler. Pour in 1 cup boiling water and mix well.

✪ Cook over medium heat, stirring constantly, until mixture thickens. Pour into piecrust.

MERINGUE:

✪ In mixing bowl, beat egg whites and cream of tartar until soft peaks form.

✪ Gradually add sugar and beat well. Spread on pie filling.

✪ Bake for 12 minutes or until meringue is golden brown. Serves 8.

Chocolate Meringue Pie

1¼ cups sugar
3 tablespoons cocoa
¼ cup flour
¼ cup (½ stick) butter, melted
3 egg yolks, slightly beaten
2¼ cups milk
1½ teaspoons vanilla
1 (10 inch) piecrust, baked

MERINGUE:
4 egg whites
⅓ cup sugar
½ teaspoon cream of tartar

✪ Preheat oven to 300°.

✪ In heavy saucepan or double boiler, combine sugar, cocoa, pinch of salt and flour.

✪ Add melted butter, egg yolks and milk and mix well. Cook on low to medium heat until mixture is creamy and thick, stirring constantly.

✪ Add vanilla and pour into baked piecrust and let set while making meringue.

MERINGUE:

✪ Beat egg whites until fairly stiff; add sugar, cream of tartar and pinch of salt; beat until stiff peaks form.

✪ Spread over chocolate mixture and form peaks of meringue with your spoon.

✪ Bake for 15 to 20 minutes or until light brown. Serves 8.

PISTACHIO-LIME PIE

2 cups vanilla wafer crumbs
¾ cup chopped pistachio nuts or pecans, divided
¼ cup (½ stick) butter
1 (8 ounce) package cream cheese, softened
1 (14 ounce) can sweetened condensed milk
¼ cup lime juice
1 (3 ounce) package instant pistachio pudding mix
1 (8 ounce) can crushed pineapple with juice
1 (8 ounce) carton whipped topping

✪ Preheat oven to 350°.

✪ Combine crumbs, ¼ cup nuts and butter and press firmly into 9-inch springform pan. Bake for 8 to 10 minutes and cool.

✪ In large mixing bowl, beat cheese until fluffy, gradually beat in sweetened condensed milk, lime juice and pudding mix and beat until smooth.

✪ Stir in ½ cup nuts and pineapple and fold in whipped topping.

✪ Pour into springform pan and refrigerate overnight. Serves 8.

PINEAPPLE-FLUFF PIE

1 (20 ounce) can crushed pineapple with juice
1 (3.4 ounce) package instant lemon pudding
1 (8 ounce) carton whipped topping
1 (9 inch) graham cracker piecrust

✪ Combine pineapple and pudding mix and beat until it thickens. Fold in whipped topping and spoon into piecrust. Refrigerate several hours. Serves 8.

★Ranch-House Buttermilk Pie

1 (10 inch) piecrust, baked, refrigerateed
4 eggs
1 cup sugar
3 tablespoons flour
2 tablespoons (¼ stick) butter, melted
3 tablespoons lemon juice
1¼ cups buttermilk
½ teaspoon lemon extract

✪ Preheat oven to 350°.

✪ In large bowl, beat eggs until light and fluffy. Gradually add sugar and blend in flour, butter and lemon juice. Add buttermilk slowly and mix until it blends well. Stir in lemon extract.

✪ Pour into piecrust; bake for 45 minutes or until knife inserted in center come out clean.

✪ Serve room temperature or refrigerated, but refrigerate any leftovers. Serves 8 to 10.

TIP: **To make buttermilk, mix 1 cup milk with 1 tablespoon lemon juice or vinegar and let milk rest for about 10 minutes.**

Strawberry Fluff Pie

1 (9-inch) piecrust, baked
1 (10 ounce) package frozen strawberries, thawed
2 egg whites
1 cup sugar
3 teaspoons lemon juice
1 (8 ounce) carton whipped topping

✪ In large mixing bowl, whip strawberries, egg whites, sugar and lemon juice. Beat at high speed for 15 minutes.

✪ Fold in whipped topping and pour into baked piecrust and freeze. Remove from freezer several minutes before slicing. Serves 8.

★TEXAS PEACH COBBLER

½ cup (1 stick) butter, melted
1 cup flour
2¼ cups sugar, divided
2 teaspoons baking powder
1 cup milk
3 to 4 cups fresh, ripe sliced peaches
1 teaspoon ground cinnamon

✪ Preheat oven to 350°.

✪ Combine butter, flour, 1 cup sugar, baking powder and ¼ teaspoon salt. Mix in milk and blend well.

✪ Spoon into sprayed 9 x 13-inch glass baking dish. Combine sliced peaches, 1¼ cups sugar and cinnamon and pour over dough.

✪ Bake for 1 hour. Crust will come to top. Serves 10 to 12.

APRICOT COBBLER

1 (20 ounce) apricot pie filling
1 (20 ounce) can crushed pineapple with juice
1 cup chopped pecans
1 (18 ounce) box yellow cake mix
1 cup (2 sticks) butter, melted
Whipped topping

✪ Preheat oven to 350°.

✪ Pour apricot pie filling into sprayed 9 x 13-inch baking dish and spread evenly.

✪ Pour crushed pineapple and juice over pie filling. Sprinkle pecans over pineapple and sprinkle cake mix over pecans.

✪ Pour melted butter over cake mix and bake for 40 minutes or until light brown and crunchy. Serve with whipped topping. Serves 10 to 12.

HOMESTEAD DATE-PECAN TARTS

1 (8 ounce) package pitted, chopped dates
1½ cups milk
½ cup flour
1½ cups sugar
3 eggs, beaten
1 teaspoon vanilla
1 cup chopped pecans
8 tart shells, baked, cooled
1 (8 ounce) carton whipping cream
3 tablespoons powdered sugar

✪ In heavy saucepan, combine dates, milk, flour and sugar and cook about 3 minutes, stirring constantly.

✪ Stir in beaten eggs and ¼ teaspoon salt and continue cooking, stirring constantly, for another 5 minutes. Stir in vanilla and pecans. Pour into baked tart shells and cool.

✪ Whip cream, add powdered sugar, top each tart with whipped cream and refrigerate. Serves 8.

Texas has the largest flock of whooping cranes in the world. The whooping crane almost became extinct and in 1937 Congress established the Aransas National Wildlife Refuge to preserve one of only two flocks left in the U.S. There are now about 150 whooping cranes that winter in Texas and summer in Canada.

PECAN TASSIES

1 (8 ounce) package cream cheese, softened
5 tablespoons butter, softened
1¾ cups flour
3 eggs, beaten
2 cups packed brown sugar
¼ cup (½ stick) butter, melted
2 teaspoons vanilla
1¾ cups coarsely chopped pecans

✪ Preheat oven to 325°.

✪ In mixing bowl, beat cream cheese and butter until light and fluffy. Add flour a little at a time and mix well.

✪ Form about 36 (1-inch) balls. Press into miniature muffin pans so sides and bottoms form tart shape.

✪ Beat eggs, brown sugar, melted butter and vanilla. Divide pecans equally into 36 tarts.

✪ Fill tarts with egg-sugar mixture and bake for 25 minutes. Cool and remove tarts from pans very carefully. Yield: 36 miniature tarts.

ORANGE BALLS

1 (12 ounce) box vanilla wafers, crushed
½ cup (1 stick) butter, melted
1 (16 ounce) box powdered sugar
1 (6 ounce) can condensed frozen orange juice
1 cup finely chopped pecans

✪ Combine wafers, butter, sugar and orange juice and mix well. Roll into balls and roll in chopped pecans. Store in airtight container. Serves 10 to 16.

★Texas Ranger Cookies

1 cup shortening
1¼ cups sugar
1 cup packed brown sugar
2 eggs
1 teaspoon vanilla
2 cups flour
1½ teaspoons baking soda
1 teaspoon baking powder
2 cups quick-cooking oatmeal
2 cups crispy rice cereal
1 (7 ounce) can flaked coconut
¾ cup chopped pecans

✪ Preheat oven to 350°.

✪ Cream shortening and both sugars. Add eggs and vanilla and mix until smooth.

✪ Sift flour, baking soda, baking powder and ½ teaspoon salt in separate bowl. Add to creamed mixture and mix well.

✪ Add oatmeal, crispy rice cereal, coconut and pecans and mix. (If mixture is crumbly, add 1 tablespoon water.)

✪ Drop dough by tablespoonfuls on baking sheet and bake for 15 minutes or until light brown. Yield: 5 dozen.

If you eat a 72-ounce steak in one hour, you can get it for free at the Big Texan Steak Ranch Restaurant in Amarillo.

No-Bake Chocolate Cookies

2 cups sugar
½ cup milk
5 heaping tablespoons cocoa
½ cup (1 stick) butter
½ cup chunky peanut butter
1 teaspoon vanilla
3 cups quick-cooking oats

✪ In saucepan, combine sugar, milk, cocoa and butter. Cook until mixture boils.

✪ Remove from heat and add peanut butter, vanilla and oats.

✪ Drop by teaspoonfuls on wax paper and cool. Do not bake! Yield: 2 dozaen cookies.

Nutty Haystacks

1 (1 pound) package orange slices
2 cups flaked coconut
1 cup chopped pecans
1 (14 ounce) can sweetened condensed milk
2 cups powdered sugar

✪ Preheat oven to 350°.

✪ Cut orange slices into small pieces and put in baking dish with coconut, pecans and milk.

✪ Bake for 10 to 15 minutes or until bubbly.

✪ Add powdered sugar and mix well. Drop by teaspoonfuls onto wax paper. Yield: 3 dozen cookies.

 *Editor's Choice*

Old-Fashion Peanut Butter Cookies

These peanut butter cookies will bring back memories and create new ones.

½ cup shortening
½ cup peanut butter
½ cup sugar
½ cup packed brown sugar
1 egg
1¼ cup flour
½ teaspoon baking powder
¾ teaspoon baking soda

✪ Preheat oven to 375°.

✪ In large bowl cream shortening, peanut butter, sugar, brown sugar and egg.

✪ In separate bowl, mix flour, baking powder, baking soda and ¼ teaspoon salt.

✪ Slowly pour flour mixture into sugar mixture and mix thoroughly.

✪ Bake until cookies are done in middle. Yield: 2 dozen cookies.

The Turkeyfest in Cuero began in 1912 when turkey buyers drove flocks of turkeys down Main Street after buying them from outlying farms. The event at one time had as many as 20,000 live turkeys in a single drive. Because some of the broad-breasted feedlot turkeys died from the exercise, the event was scaled back to include hardy range-raised turkeys in a Great Gobbler Gallop.

★Cowboy Cookies

2 cups flour
1 teaspoon baking soda
½ teaspoon baking powder
1 cup (2 sticks) butter, softened
1 cup sugar
1 cup packed brown sugar
2 eggs
1 teaspoon vanilla
2 cups quick-cooking oats
1 (6 ounce) package chocolate chips
1 cup chopped pecans

✪ Preheat oven to 350°.

✪ Combine flour, baking soda, baking powder and ½ teaspoon salt in large bowl and set aside.

✪ In separate bowl, cream butter, both sugars, eggs and vanilla until fluffy.

✪ Add flour mixture and mix well.

✪ Add oats, chocolate chips and pecans and mix well.

✪ Drop by teaspoonfuls on sprayed cookie sheet and bake for 15 minutes. Yield: 3 dozen cookies.

The largest collection of vintage World War II aircraft in the world is maintained by the Confederate Air Force of Texas and is located in the American Airpower Heritage Museum in Midland.

 *Editor's Choice*

BAYLOR COOKIES

The best "ice box" cookies around.

1 cup shortening
¼ cup packed brown sugar
1 cup sugar
1 egg
1½ teaspoons vanilla
2 cups flour
2 teaspoons baking powder
1 cup chopped pecans

✪ Preheat oven to 350°.

✪ Combine shortening, both sugars, egg, ¼ teaspoon salt and vanilla and mix well.

✪ Add flour and baking powder and mix until it blends well. Add pecans and mix.

✪ Divide dough in half and roll in log shapes on sheet of floured wax paper.

✪ Place rolled dough on another piece of wax paper and roll up. Refrigerate rolls several hours.

✪ When dough is thoroughly refrigerateed, slice in ½-inch slices.

✪ Bake on cookie sheet for 15 minutes or until slightly brown. Yield: 3 dozen cookies.

Choc-O-Cherry Cookies

½ cup (1 stick) butter, softened
1 cup sugar
1 egg
½ teaspoon vanilla
1½ cups flour
½ cup cocoa
¼ teaspoon baking powder
¼ teaspoon baking soda
1 (6 ounce) package chocolate chips
1 (10 ounce) jar maraschino cherries, well drained

✪ Preheat oven to 350°.

✪ Cream butter, sugar, egg and vanilla until light and fluffy.

✪ Add dry ingredients and ¼ teaspoon salt and mix.

✪ Add chocolate chips and cherries cut in fourths and mix.

✪ Drop by teaspoonfuls on cookie sheet and bake for 15 minutes.
Yield: 2 dozen cookies.

The Texas State Capitol building has more square footage than any other state capitol building.

★Big-as-Texas Cookies

1½ cups sugar
1 cup packed brown sugar
1¾ cups flour
2 teaspoons baking powder
1 teaspoon baking soda
¾ teaspoon ground cinnamon
¼ teaspoon ground nutmeg
3 cups quick-cooking oats
1 cup oil
2 eggs, beaten
5 tablespoons milk
1 cup chopped pecans
1 (6 ounce) package milk chocolate chips

✪ Preheat oven to 375°.

✪ In large bowl, combine both sugars, flour, baking powder, baking soda, spices, ½ teaspoon salt and oats and mix well.

✪ Add oil, eggs and milk and mix well. Stir in pecans and chocolate chips. (Mixture will be stiff.)

✪ Drop by heaping tablespoonfuls or bigger on unsprayed cookie sheets. Bake for 10 to 13 minutes. Yield: 2 dozen cookies.

The San Jacinto Monument near Houston is the tallest monumental column in the world. It commemorates the battle of San Jacinto assuring Texas of its independence from Mexico.

Texas Butter Cookies

1 cup (2 sticks) butter, softened
1 (16 ounce) box powdered sugar
1 egg
1 teaspoon almond extract
1 teaspoon vanilla
2½ cups plus 1 tablespoon flour
¾ teaspoon cream of tartar
1 teaspoon baking soda

✪ With mixer, cream butter, powdered sugar and add egg, vanilla and almond extract and mix well.

✪ In separate bowl, sift flour, cream of tartar and baking soda and add to creamed mixture. Cover and refrigerate several hours.

✪ When ready to bake, preheat oven to 350°.

✪ Roll cookie dough into ¼-inch thickness and use cookie cutters to make desired shapes. Place on unsprayed cookie sheet.

✪ Bake for 7 to 8 minutes, but do not brown. Sprinkle a little granulated sugar over each cookie while still hot. Yield: 2 dozen cookies.

Surprise Chocolates

2 pounds white chocolate
2 cups Spanish peanuts
2 cups small pretzels sticks, broken

✪ Melt chocolate in double boiler. Stir in peanuts and pretzels.

✪ Drop by teaspoonfuls on wax paper. Work fast because mixture hardens quickly.

✪ Place in freezer for 1 hour before storing. Yield: About 5 dozen.

Sierra Nuggets

1 cup (2 sticks) butter, softened
1 cup packed brown sugar
1½ cups sugar
1 tablespoon milk
2 teaspoons vanilla
2 eggs
1 cup crushed corn flakes
3 cups quick-cooking oats
1½ cups flour
1 teaspoon baking soda
2 teaspoons ground cinnamon
¼ teaspoon ground nutmeg
⅛ teaspoon ground cloves
½ cup flaked coconut
2 cups chocolate chips
1 cup chopped pecans

✪ Preheat oven to 350°.

✪ In large mixing bowl, cream butter and both sugars and beat in milk, vanilla and eggs. Stir in corn flakes and oatmeal.

✪ Sift flour, baking soda, 1 teaspoon salt and spices. Gradually add to cookie mixture. (Cookie batter will be very stiff.)

✪ Stir in coconut, chocolate chips and pecans. Drop by teaspoonfuls onto cookie sheet. Bake for 10 to 15 minutes. Yield: 5 dozen cookies.

Shortbread Crunchies

1 cup (2 sticks) butter, softened
1 cup oil
1 cup sugar
1 cup packed brown sugar
1 egg
1 teaspoon vanilla
1 cup quick-cooking oats
3½ cups flour
1 teaspoon baking soda
1 cup crushed cornflakes
1 (7 ounce) can flaked coconut
1 cup chopped pecans

✪ Preheat oven to 325°.

✪ Cream butter, oil and both sugars. Add egg and vanilla and mix well.

✪ Add oats, flour, baking soda and 1 teaspoon salt and mix. Add cornflakes, coconut and pecans and mix.

✪ Drop by teaspoonfuls on unsprayed baking sheet. Flatten with fork dipped in water.

✪ Bake for 15 minutes or until light brown. Yield: 4 dozen cookies.

The largest equestrian sculpture in the world is the Mustangs of Las Colinas located near Dallas-Fort Worth International Airport.

 *Editor's Choice*

CHEERLEADER BROWNIES
Great, chewy, chocolaty brownies! They won't last long!

⅔ cup oil
2 cups sugar
4 eggs, beaten
⅓ cup corn syrup
½ cup cocoa
1½ cups flour
1 teaspoon baking powder
2 teaspoons vanilla
1 cup chopped pecans

✪ Preheat oven to 350°.

✪ In large bowl, mix oil, sugar, eggs and corn syrup.

✪ In separate bowl, mix cocoa, flour, 1 teaspoon salt and baking powder.

✪ Slowly pour cocoa mixture into sugar mixture and mix thoroughly. Stir in vanilla and chopped pecans.

✪ Pour into sprayed 9 x 13-inch baking pan and bake for about 50 minutes or until toothpick inserted in center comes out clean. Yield: 12 to 14 brownies.

According to newspaper accounts, Jacob Brodbeck flew an airplane powered by coil springs to tree-top heights in 1865, 40 years before the Wright Brothers flew in 1903. Shortly after achieving tree-top height, he crashed into a henhouse killing several chickens and scaring several others to death.

GLAZED-BUTTERSCOTCH BROWNIES

3 cups packed brown sugar
1 cup (2 sticks) butter, softened
3 eggs
3 cups flour
2 tablespoons baking powder
1½ cups chopped pecans
1 (7 ounce) can flaked coconut

GLAZE:
½ cup packed brown sugar
⅓ cup evaporated milk
½ cup (1 stick) butter
1 cup powdered sugar
½ teaspoon vanilla

✪ Preheat oven to 350°.

✪ Combine and beat sugar and butter until fluffy. Add eggs and blend.

✪ Combine flour, baking powder and ½ teaspoon salt and add to sugar-egg mixture, 1 cup at a time. Add pecans and coconut.

✪ Spread batter in 10 x 15-inch well sprayed baking pan and bake for 20 to 25 minutes. Batter will be hard to spread.

✪ For glaze, combine brown sugar, milk, butter and ⅛ teaspoon salt in saucepan and bring to boil.

✪ Cool slightly and add powdered sugar and vanilla and beat until smooth. Spread glaze over cooled brownies. Yield: 14 to 18 brownies.

MILLION-DOLLAR BARS

½ cup (1 stick) butter
2 cups graham cracker crumbs
1 (6 ounce) package chocolate chips
1 (6 ounce) package butterscotch chips
1 cup chopped pecans
1 (7 ounce) can flaked coconut
1 (14 ounce) can sweetened condensed milk

✪ Preheat oven to 325°.

✪ Melt butter in sprayed 9 x 13-inch baking dish.

✪ Sprinkle crumbs over butter and stir. Add layers of chocolate chips,
butterscotch chips, pecans and coconut.

✪ Pour sweetened condensed milk over top and bake for about 30
minutes. Cool in pan and cut bars. Yield: 12 to 14 bars.

YUMMY CHESS SQUARES

1 (18 ounce) box butter cake mix
4 eggs, divided
½ cup (1 stick) butter, melted
2 teaspoons vanilla, divided
1 (8 ounce) package cream cheese, softened
1 (1 pound) box powdered sugar

✪ Preheat oven to 300°.

✪ Combine cake mix, 1 egg, butter and 1 teaspoon vanilla and mix well.
Batter will be very thick.

✪ Spread in sprayed, floured 9 x 13-inch baking dish.

✪ Combine remaining 3 eggs, 1 teaspoon vanilla, cream cheese and
powdered sugar and beat well. Spread over cake mixture. Bake for
1 hour. Refrigerate and serve. Yield: 12 to 14 squares.

CHOCOLATE-STREUSEL BARS

1¾ cups unsifted flour
1½ cups powdered sugar
½ cup cocoa
1 cup (2 sticks) butter, softened
1 (8-ounce) package cream cheese, softened
1 (14-ounce) can sweetened condensed milk
1 egg
2 teaspoons vanilla
⅓ cup chopped pecans

✪ Preheat oven to 350°.

✪ In large bowl, combine flour, sugar and cocoa. Cut in butter until crumbly.

✪ Reserve 1 cup crumb mixture and press remaining dough firmly in sprayed 9 x 13-inch baking pan. Bake for 15 minutes.

✪ In large mixing bowl, beat cream cheese until fluffy. Gradually beat in condensed milk until smooth.

✪ Add egg and vanilla and mix well. Pour over prepared crust.

✪ Combine pecans with reserved crumb mixture and sprinkle over cream cheese mixture.

✪ Bake for 25 minutes or until bubbly.

✪ Cool and refrigerate. Cut into bars and store in covered container. Yield: 12 to 14 bars.

BUTTER-PECAN TURTLE BARS

2 cups flour
1½ cups packed light brown sugar, divided
1 cup plus 2 tablespoons(2¼ sticks) butter, divided
1½ cups chopped pecans
4 (1 ounce) squares semi-sweet chocolate

✪ Preheat oven to 350°.

✪ Melt ½ cup (1 stick) butter and combine with flour and ¾ cup brown sugar in large mixing bowl and blend until crumbly.

✪ Pat firmly into sprayed 9 x 13-inch baking pan. Sprinkle pecans over unbaked crust and set aside.

✪ In small saucepan, combine ¾ cup brown sugar and 6 tablespoons (¾ stick) butter. Cook over medium heat, stirring constantly.

✪ When mixture comes to boil, boil for 1 minute, stirring constantly. Drizzle caramel sauce over pecans and crust.

✪ Bake for 18 to 20 minutes or until caramel layer is bubbly. Remove from oven and cool.

✪ In saucepan over low heat, melt chocolate squares and ¼ cup (½ stick) butter and stir until smooth. Pour over bars and spread around evenly. Cool and cut into bars. Yield: 12 to 14 bars.

★TEXAS PECAN BARS

CRUST:
3 cups flour
¾ cup (1½ sticks) butter, softened
⅓ cup sugar

FILLING:
4 eggs, beaten
1½ cups packed brown sugar
1½ cups light corn syrup
3 tablespoons butter, melted
1½ teaspoons vanilla
2½ cups chopped pecans

✪ Preheat oven to 350°.

✪ With mixer, blend flour, butter, sugar and ¾ teaspoon salt and press firmly in sprayed 12 x 18-inch jelly-roll pan.

✪ Bake for 25 minutes or until golden brown.

✪ For filling mix all ingredients except pecans. Spread pecans over crust, pour in egg mixture and spread evenly.

✪ Bake for 25 more minutes or until filling sets. Cool and cut into squares. Yield: 12 to 14 bars.

CHEESECAKE-PECAN BARS

1 cup flour
5 tablespoons butter, softened
½ cup packed brown sugar
1 (8 ounce) package cream cheese, softened
1 egg
1 tablespoon milk
½ teaspoon vanilla
½ cup chopped pecans

✪ Preheat oven to 350°.

✪ In bowl, combine flour, butter and brown sugar. Press into unsprayed 8 x 8-inch baking pan. Bake for 10 minutes.

✪ With mixer, beat cream cheese, egg, milk and vanilla until smooth and scrape sides of bowl often.

✪ Spread over baked flour layer and sprinkle with pecans.

✪ Bake for 25 minutes. Cool and refrigerate at least 2 hours before cutting into bars. Store in refrigerator. Yield: 8 to 9 bars.

Texas is the largest oil producer in the U.S.

CARMELITAS

CRUST:
1 cup flour
¾ cup packed brown sugar
1 cup quick-cooking oats
½ teaspoon baking soda
¾ cup (1½ sticks) butter, melted

FILLING:
1 (6 ounce) package chocolate chips
¾ cup chopped pecans
1 (12 ounce) jar caramel ice cream topping
3 tablespoons flour

✪ Preheat oven to 350°.

✪ Combine ⅛ teaspoon salt and all crust ingredients in large mixing bowl and blend well with mixer to form crumbs.

✪ Press two-thirds crumbs into sprayed 9 x 13-inch baking pan. Bake for 10 minutes.

✪ Remove from oven and sprinkle with chocolate chips and pecans.

✪ Blend caramel topping with flour and 1 to 2 tablespoons water and spread over chips and pecans. Sprinkle with remaining crumb mixture.

✪ Bake for 20 minutes or until golden brown. Refrigerate for 2 hours before cutting into squares. Yield: 12 to 14 squares.

ICED PINEAPPLE SQUARES

1½ cups sugar
2 cups flour
1½ teaspoons baking soda
1 (15 ounce) can crushed pineapple, drained
2 eggs

FROSTING:
1½ cups sugar
½ cup (1 stick) butter
1 (5 ounce) can evaporated milk
1 cup chopped pecans
1 (7 ounce) can flaked coconut
1 teaspoon vanilla

✪ Preheat oven to 350°.

✪ Mix sugar, flour, baking soda, ½ teaspoon salt, pineapple and eggs.

✪ Pour into sprayed, floured 9 x 13-inch baking dish.

FROSTING:

✪ Mix sugar, butter and evaporated milk in saucepan and boil 4 minutes, stirring constantly.

✪ Remove from heat and add pecans, coconut and vanilla. Spread over hot squares. Yield: 12 squares.

BUNUELOS

4 cups flour
3 tablespoons sugar
1 teaspoon baking powder
2 eggs, well beaten
1 cup milk
½ cup (1 stick) butter, melted
1 teaspoon ground cinnamon
1 cup sugar

✪ In large bowl combine flour, sugar, 1 teaspoon salt and baking powder. Combine well beaten eggs and milk and gradually stir into flour mixture. Add melted butter and mix well.

✪ Place dough on lightly floured board and knead until dough is smooth and elastic. Pinch off about 2 tablespoons dough and make balls. Flatten balls to 4 x 4-inch squares.

✪ Deep fry flattened balls until light brown on both sides. Drain on paper towels and sprinkle with mixture of cinnamon and sugar. Serves 15 to 20.

Texas is the leading producer of jalapenos in the U.S. Texas produces more than 50% of all jalapenos consumed in the U.S.

A mild jalapeno was introduced in 1991 and developed by a chili-producing professor at Texas A&M University.

SOPAPILLAS

4 cups sifted flour
1 tablespoon baking powder
3 tablespoons sugar
3 tablespoons shortening
1¼ cups milk
Oil for deep frying

✪ Combine flour, 1 teaspoon salt, baking powder and sugar. Cut in shortening and add just enough milk to make dough firm enough to roll. Cover bowl and let stand for about 45 minutes.

✪ Roll ¼-inch thick on lightly floured board and cut into diamond-shaped pieces.

✪ Heat enough oil in heavy pot for frying. Fry a few pieces at a time, turn at once so they will puff evenly, then brown on both sides.

✪ Drain on paper towels and serve with butter. Serves 15 to 20.

MANGO CREAM

2 ripe, soft mangoes
½ gallon vanilla ice cream, softened
1 (6 ounce) can frozen lemonade, thawed
1 (8 ounce) carton whipped topping

✪ Peel mangoes, cut slices around seed and chop slices. In large bowl, mix ice cream, lemonade and whipped topping and fold in mango chunks.

✪ Quickly spoon mixture into parfait glasses, cover with plastic wrap and freeze. Serves 8 to 10.

★FLAN
This is a Mexican custard served at most Tex-Mex restaurants.

2 tablespoons butter
1 cup sugar, divided
1 (14 ounce) can sweetened condensed milk
1 (13 ounce) can evaporated milk
4 eggs, very well beaten
1 teaspoon vanilla

✪ Preheat oven to 350°.

✪ In heavy saucepan, rub butter on bottom and sides.

✪ In saucepan over medium heat, melt ½ cup sugar until it carmelizes. Add remaining sugar and stir until there is clear brown syrup. Pour equal parts into 6 individual custard bowls.

✪ Combine condensed milk, evaporated milk, eggs and vanilla and mix well. Pour mixture over cooled, melted sugar mixture in custard bowls.

✪ Place bowls in another container half-filled with water.

✪ Bake for 1 hour. Flan is done when toothpick comes out clean.

✪ Serve by carefully turning bowls upside down onto plate and removing flan from bowls. The caramelized sugar will be on top. Serves 6.

OLD-FASHION ICE CREAM

4 large eggs, separated
2 tablespoons flour
2¾ cups sugar
1 tablespoon vanilla
3 quarts milk, divided
1 pint whipping cream
Chipped ice
Rock salt
1-gallon freezer container

✪ In mixing bowl, beat egg yolks until light and fluffy.

✪ Combine flour and sugar, add to egg yolks and 1 quart milk and beat well.

✪ Beat egg whites until stiff and fold into yolk-milk mixture. Pour into double boiler and heat, stirring constantly, until mixture thickens. Pour into ice cream freezer.

✪ Add whipping cream and enough milk to reach 3 inches from top of freezer. Cover tightly and pack freezer with ice and rock salt and freeze. Serves 10 to 14.

TIP: To make peach or banana ice cream, add 2 cups diced fruit before adding remaining milk.

AFTER-DINNER KAHLUA ICE

1 pint vanilla ice cream
⅓ cup Kahlua® liqueur
¼ cup creme de cacao liqueur
½ cup milk
Crushed ice, optional

✪ Place scoops of ice cream in blender and add liqueurs and milk.

✪ Process in blender until smooth and add crushed ice if desired.

✪ Pour mixture in serving glasses and serve immediately. Serves 4 to 6.

KAHLUA SOUFFLE

1 tablespoon cornstarch
1 cup half-and-half cream, divided
3 egg yolks
6 tablespoons sugar, divided
1 tablespoon unflavored gelatin
½ cup Kahlua® liqueur
½ teaspoon vanilla
3 egg whites

✪ In bowl, combine cornstarch and small amount of half-and-half cream and blend well.

✪ Add remaining half-and-half cream and cook over low heat, stirring constantly, until mixture thickens. Beat egg yolks lightly with 5 tablespoons sugar.

✪ Soften gelatin in ¼ cup water, add yolks and gelatin to half-and-half cream mixture and cook, stirring constantly, an additional 4 to 5 minutes.

✪ Cool slightly and add Kahlua and vanilla.

✪ Beat egg whites until very stiff and add remaining 1 tablespoon sugar and pinch of salt.

✪ Fold egg whites into yolk mixture, pour into souffle dish and refrigerate. Serves 4 to 6.

CREAMY BANANA PUDDING

1 (14 ounce) can sweetened condensed milk
1 (3¾ ounce) package instant vanilla pudding mix
1 (8-ounce) carton whipped topping
36 vanilla wafers
3 bananas, sliced, dipped in lemon juice

✪ In large bowl, combine sweetened condensed milk and 1½ cups cold water.

✪ Add pudding mix and beat well and refrigerate 5 minutes.

✪ Fold in whipped topping. Spoon 1 cup pudding mixture into 2½-quart glass serving bowl.

✪ Top with one-third each of wafers, bananas and pudding. Repeat layers twice and end with pudding.

✪ Cover, refrigerate and store in covered container in refrigerator. Serves 10 to 12.

More than 100 species of cacti grow in Texas, the widest assortment of any other state in the U.S. Cacti are used in Texas for foods in salads, wines and jelly. The tunas or seed pods of the prickly pear are used in salads, wines and jelly. The pads or nopalitos with their spines singed off are used in a small way in Tex-Mex food and a big way for cattle.

LEMON LUSH

1¼ cups flour
⅔ cup butter
½ cup chopped pecans
1 cup powdered sugar
1 (8 ounce) package cream cheese, softened
1 (12 ounce) carton whipped topping, divided
2 (3¾ ounce) package instant lemon pudding
1 tablespoon lemon juice
2¾ cups milk

✪ Preheat oven to 375°.

✪ Mix flour, butter and pecans. Pat into sprayed 9 x 13-inch baking dish and bake for 15 minutes. Cool.

✪ Beat powdered sugar and cream cheese until fluffy and fold in 2 cups whipped topping. Spread on nut crust.

✪ Mix pudding, lemon juice and milk, beat and spread over second layer. Top with remaining whipped topping and refrigerate. To serve, cut into squares. Serves 9 to 12.

TEXAS FOOD FESTIVALS

Texas Citrus Festival	Mission	January
Wild Hog Festival	Sabinal	February
Oysterfest	Fulton	March
Fiesta	San Antonio	April
Strawberry Festival	Poteet	April
Annual Electra Goat Barbecue	Electra	May
Annual Crayfish Festival	Bandera	May
Annual Chuck Wagon Gathering	Lubbock	May
Watermelon Thump	Luling	June
Texas Blueberry Festival	Nacogdoches	June
Onion Fest	Noonday	June
Night in Old Pecos Cantaloupe Festival	Pecos	June
Peach JAMboree	Stonewall	June

Margarita-Party Dessert

½ cup (1 stick) butter
1 (12 ounce) box vanilla wafers, crushed
3 quarts vanilla ice cream, softened
1 (6 ounce) can frozen limeade concentrate, thawed
½ cup tequila
2 tablespoons cointreau liqueur
Juice of 1 lime
½ teaspoon grated lime peel
1 lime

✪ Melt butter in 9 x 13-inch glass dish, place crushed wafers in dish and mix well. Pat down to make crust.

✪ In large mixing bowl, combine softened ice cream, limeade concentrate, tequila, cointreau, lime juice and lime peel. Fold together and mix well. Pour over vanilla wafer crumbs and freeze.

✪ To serve, slice in squares. When ready to serve, slice lime very thin. Make cut to center of each lime slice, twist and place on each serving for garnish. Serves 9 to 12.

TEXAS FOOD FESTIVALS

Black-Eyed Pea Jamboree	Athens	July
Parker County Peach Festival	Weatherford	July
Chronicle Hot Sauce Festival	Austin	August
Great Texas Peanut Festival	Gorman	September
Texas Pecan Festival	Groves	September
Kolache Fest	Hallettsville	September
Tomato Fest	Jacksonville	September
Turkeyfest	Cuero	October
Hot Pepper Festival	Palestine	October
Texas Rice Festival	Winnie	October
Punkin Days	Floydada	October
Spinach Festival	Crystal City	November
Chili Pepperama	Dallas	November

FRUIT FAJITAS

1 (20 ounce) can cherry pie filling
10 small flour tortillas
1½ cups sugar
¾ cup (1½ sticks) butter
1 teaspoon almond flavoring

✪ Preheat oven to 350°.

✪ Divide pie filling equally on flour tortillas. Roll up and place in sprayed 9 x 13-inch baking dish.

✪ In saucepan, mix 1 cup water, sugar and butter and bring to boil. Add almond flavoring and pour over flour tortillas.

✪ Place tortilla rolls in refrigerator and soak 1 to 24 hours.

✪ Bake for 20 to 25 minutes until brown and bubbly.

✪ Serve hot or room temperature with spoonful whipped topping. Serves 8.

TIP: Other pie fillings may be used in place of cherry pie filling.

★TEXAS MILLIONAIRES

1 (16 ounce) package pecan halves
2 (12 ounce) packages chocolate chips
1 (7 ounce) jar marshmallow creme
5 cups sugar
½ cup (1 stick) butter
1 (13 ounce) can evaporated milk

✪ In bowl, combine and mix pecans, chocolate chips and marshmallow creme and set aside.

✪ In saucepan, mix sugar, butter and evaporated milk. Heat to rolling boil, stir constantly and cook for 7 minutes.

✪ Pour over pecan-chocolate chip mixture and stir until mixture blends well.

✪ Drop by tablespoonfuls on wax paper; allow millionaires to set and become firm before serving. Store in airtight container in refrigerator. Serves 12 to 16.

PEANUT CLUSTERS

1 (24 ounce) package almond bark
1 (12 ounce) package milk chocolate chips
5 cups salted peanuts

✪ In double boiler, melt almond bark and chocolate chips. Stir in peanuts and drop by teaspoonfuls onto wax paper. Store in airtight container. Serves 8 to 12.

Editor's Choice

★TEXAS PEANUT BRITTLE

3 cups sugar
1 cup light corn syrup
3 cups raw shelled peanuts
1½ tablespoons butter
2 teaspoons baking soda

✪ In heavy skillet, combine sugar, ½ cup water and corn syrup and boil until soft-boil or until it spins a thread.

✪ Add peanuts, stirring constantly, until mixture turns brownish gold.

✪ Remove from heat, add butter, baking soda and ½ teaspoon salt. (Mixture will bubble up.) Immediately pour onto sprayed cookie sheet to cool.

✪ When cool, break into serving-size pieces. Serves 10 to 15.

TUMBLEWEEDS

1 (12 ounce) package butterscotch chips
¼ cup peanut butter
1 (12 ounce) can peanuts
1 (4 ounce) can shoestring potatoes

✪ In saucepan on low heat, melt chips with peanut butter and mix well.

✪ Stir in peanuts and shoestring potatoes. Drop by tablespoonfuls on wax paper. Store in airtight container. Serves 8 to 12.

TEX-MEX PRALINES

2½ cups sugar
1 (5 ounce) can evaporated milk
3 tablespoons white corn syrup
2 tablespoons butter
2 cups pecan halves

✪ In large saucepan, combine sugar, milk, corn syrup and butter and bring to boil.

✪ Add pecans and cook on high until candy is at soft-boil stage (238° on candy thermometer).

✪ Remove from heat and beat until creamy. Drop by tablespoons on wax paper. Serves 8 to 12.

─────◈─────

MEXICAN-PECAN PRALINES

1 (16 ounce) box light brown sugar
2 cups whole pecans
3 tablespoons light corn syrup
½ cup sweetened condensed milk
½ cup (1 stick) butter
½ teaspoon cream of tartar

✪ In heavy saucepan, combine all ingredients and cook over medium heat, stirring constantly, until mixture reaches hard-boil stage (250°).

✪ Remove from heat and beat until candy thickens, about 4 to 5 minutes.

✪ Drop by tablespoonfuls onto wax paper and cool. Serves 8 to 12.

─────◈─────

★TEXAS CREAMY PRALINES

2¼ cups sugar
1 (3 ounce) can evaporated milk
½ cup white corn syrup
¼ teaspoon baking soda
¼ cup (½ stick) butter
1 teaspoon vanilla
2 cups chopped pecans

✪ Mix sugar, evaporated milk, corn syrup and baking soda and cook in double boiler.

✪ Stir constantly and cook until ball forms when dripped in cold water or until it reaches soft-boil stage on candy thermometer. This will take about 15 minutes.

✪ Remove from heat and add butter, vanilla and pecans and beat until it is cool and stiff enough to keep its shape when poured on wax paper. This may take 15 to 20 minutes of beating.

✪ Pour on wax paper in desired size and cool completely. Store in airtight container or wrap individually in plastic wrap. Serves 8 to 12.

Space Center Houston is the visitor's center for NASA's Johnson Space Center. Interactive displays and simulators give visitors the feel of working in space and landing the lunar orbiter.

Editor's Choice

★CREAMY PRALINES

1¼ cups sugar
1¼ cups light corn syrup
1 cup (2 sticks) butter
1 (8 ounce) carton whipping cream
4 to 5 cups pecan halves
2 teaspoons vanilla

❂ In heavy saucepan, combine sugar and corn syrup. Cook until mixture is soft-boil stage (240°).

❂ Add butter and cream, bring to boil and cook, stirring constantly, until candy reaches hard-boil stage (250°).

❂ Remove from heat and stir in pecans and vanilla. Beat candy vigorously until candy is fairly cool.

❂ Drop by tablespoonfuls onto wax paper or foil. Let candy stand for 1 to 2 hours and wrap each piece separately in plastic wrap. Serves 8 to 12.

WHITE CHOCOLATE FUDGE

1 (8 ounce) package cream cheese, softened
4 cups powdered sugar
1½ teaspoons vanilla
12 ounces almond bark, melted
¾ cup chopped pecans

❂ Beat cream cheese at medium speed until smooth, gradually add sugar and vanilla and beat well to mix. Stir in melted almond bark and pecans. Spread into sprayed 8-inch square pan. Refrigerate until firm. Yield: 12 squares.

★SWEET POTATO PUDDING

This recipe is so old it came with the wagon trains.

4 large sweet potatoes, peeled, finely shredded
1 cup buttermilk
2 (12 ounce) cans evaporated milk
2 cups sugar
1½ cups (3 sticks) butter, melted
1 teaspoon ground nutmeg
1 teaspoon ground cinnamon
1 teaspoon baking soda

✪ Preheat oven to 350°.

✪ Place sweet potatoes in large, covered ovenproof dish.

✪ Pour buttermilk and evaporated milk over sweet potatoes immediately after shredding so they will not change color.

✪ Stir in sugar, butter, nutmeg and cinnamon. Add baking soda and stir slightly.

✪ Bake for 1 hour 30 minutes. Serve hot. Serves 12.

TIP: My grandfather shredded sweet potatoes by hand for this recipe and it was no easy task, but plenty worth it.

HOMEMADE PLUM JELLY

5 to 6 pounds tart plums
(5½ cups plum juice)
1 (1.75 ounce) package Sure-Jell®
6½ cups sugar

✪ Wash and place plums in very large roasting pan or pot and cover with water. Boil until plums are soft and mushy and stir often. Watch carefully to keep pan from boiling over.

✪ Pour plums and juice into large colander with large pan to catch juice. You should have 5½ cups juice. Add up to ½ cup water, if necessary to have exactly 5½ cups juice.

✪ In large roasting pan place juice and envelope of Sure-Jell and bring to boil (again watch for spillage).

✪ Add sugar, return to a full rolling boil (a boil that doesn't stop bubbling when stirred), and stir constantly. Boil for exactly 1 minute.

✪ Remove from heat and skim off any foam with metal spoon. Ladle quickly into sterilized jars, filling to within ⅛ inch of top of jars.

✪ Cover with two-piece lids and screw bands on tightly. Let stand at room temperature at least 24 hours. Refrigerate after jars are opened. Yield: 6 half-pint jars.

TIP: Using this Sure-Jell method, measure must be EXACTLY 5½ cups juice and 6½ cups sugar.

BIBLIOGRAPHY

Jane Butel, *Chili Madness*, New York, NY, 1980

Alice Guadalupe Tapp, *Tamales 101*, Berkeley. Ca, 2002

Maria Teresa Bermudez, *Mexican Family Favorites Cookbook*, Phoenix, Az, 1983

Junior League of Corpus Christi, *Fiesta*, Corpus Christi, Tx., 1973

Blue-Lake-Deerhaven Cookbook Committee, *A Texas Hill Country Cookbook*, Marble Falls, Tx. 1976

The Richardson Woman's Club, *The Texas Experience*, Richardson, Tx. 1982

The Junior League of San Antonio, *Flavors*, San Antonio, Tx. 1978

Harris Farms Publishing, *Mama's Cooking*, Hamilton, Tx. 1977

Houston Junior League, *Houston Junior League Cookbook*, Houston, Tx. 1968

Anne Dingus, *More Texas Sayings*, Houston, Tx. 1966

W. C. Jameson, *Bubba Speak Texas Folk Sayings*, Okano, Tx. 1998

James Troman, *Down-Home Texas Cooking*, Houston, Tx. 1982

Houston Junior Forum, *Buffet on the Bayou*, Houston, Tx 1993

The Junior League of Corpus Chrisiti, *Viva Tradiciones*, Cropus Christi, Tx. 1996

Louise P. Grace, *R.D. Leaving Home*, Bonham, Tx 1984

H.E. Butt Grocery Company, *Texas Favorites*, Austin, Tx 1985

Jean Coates, *The Ultimate Cooking with 4 Ingredients*, Highland Village, Tx. 2002

Sheryn & Barbara Jones, *Mother's Recipes*, Highland Village, Tx. 2002

Barbara C. Jones, *Cooking with 5 Ingredients*, Highland Village, Tx. 2002

Longhorn Breeders Association, *Texas Longhorn Cookbook*, Fort Worth, Tx.. 1998

Austin Junior Forum, *Best of Lone Star Legacy*, Highland Village, Tx. 2001

Texas A & M University, *Texas Almanac*, Dallas, Tx. 2004

Wiley Publishing, Inc., *Frommers's Texas*, New York, NY 2003

Larry D. Hodge, *Good Times in Texas*, Plano, Tx 1999

Fixin's!

ALPHABETICAL INDEX AND CROSS REFERENCE

Official Vegetable of The State of Texas

TEXAS 1015 SUPER-SWEET ONION

⇥⇥⇥ Slim's Tidbit: ⇤⇤⇤

"Time to put the chairs in the wagon."

Cookbooks Published by Cookbook Resources, LLC

Bringing Family and Friends to the Table

The Best of Cooking with 3 Ingredients

The Ultimate Cooking
with 4 Ingredients

Easy Cooking with 5 Ingredients

Diabetic Cooking with 4 Ingredients

Healthy Cooking with 4 Ingredients

Gourmet Cooking with 5 Ingredients

4-Ingredient Recipes
for 30-Minute Meals

Essential 3-4-5 Ingredient Cookbook

The Best 1001 Short, Easy Recipes

1001 Fast Easy Recipes

Busy Woman's Quick & Easy Recipes

Busy Woman's Slow Cooker Recipes

Easy Slow Cooker Cookbook

Easy One-Dish Meals

Easy Potluck Recipes

Easy Casseroles

Easy Desserts

Sunday Night Suppers

Easy Church Suppers

365 Easy Meals

365 Easy Chicken Recipes

365 Easy Soups and Stews

Quick Fixes with Cake Mixes

Kitchen Keepsakes/More
Kitchen Keepsakes

Gifts for the Cookie Jar

All New Gifts for the Cookie Jar

Muffins In A Jar

Brownies In A Jar

Gifts In A Pickle Jar

The Big Bake Sale Cookbook

Classic Tex-Mex and Texas Cooking

Classic Southwest Cooking

Southern Family Favorites

Miss Sadie's Southern Cooking

The Great Canadian Cookbook

Texas Longhorn Cookbook

Cookbook 25 Years

The Best of Lone Star Legacy Cookbook

A Little Taste of Texas

A Little Taste of Texas II

Trophy Hunters' Wild Game Cookbook

Italian Family Cookbook

Old-Fashioned Cookies

Grandmother's Cookies

Quilters' Cooking Companion

Mother's Recipes

Recipe Keeper

Cookie Dough Secrets

Casseroles to the Rescue

Texas Longhorn Cookbook

Holiday Recipes

Mealtimes and Memories

Southwest Sizzler

Southwest Olé

Class Treats

Leaving Home

www.cookbookresources.com

cookbook resources LLC

Your Ultimate Source for Easy Cookbooks

To Order: **Classic Tex-Mex and Texas Cooking**

Please send ___ copies @ $19.95 (U.S.) each $ _____

Texas residents add sales tax @ $1.65 each $ _____

Plus postage/handling @ $6.00 (1ˢᵗ copy) $ _____

$1.00 (each additional copy) $ _____

Check or Credit Card (Canada-credit card only) Total $ _____

Charge to: ☐ MasterCard   ☐ VISA   Expiration Date └─┴─┘└─┴─┘ (mm/yy)

Account No. └─┴─┴─┴─┘└─┴─┴─┴─┘└─┴─┴─┴─┘└─┴─┴─┴─┘

Signature _____

Name (please print) _____

Address _____

City _____ State/Prov. _____ Zip/Postal Code _____

Telephone (Day) _____ (Evening) _____

Order online at www.cookbookresources.com — or

Mail to: Cookbook Resources   Call Toll Free: (866) 229-2665
       541 Doubletree Drive
       Highland Village, Texas 75077   Fax: (972) 317-6404

---

o Order: **Classic Tex-Mex and Texas Cooking**

Please send ___ copies @ $19.95 (U.S.) each $ _____

Texas residents add sales tax @ $1.65 each $ _____

Plus postage/handling @ $6.00 (1ˢᵗ copy) $ _____

$1.00 (each additional copy) $ _____

Check or Credit Card (Canada-credit card only) Total $ _____

Charge to: ☐ MasterCard   ☐ VISA   Expiration Date └─┴─┘└─┴─┘ (mm/yy)

Account No. └─┴─┴─┴─┘└─┴─┴─┴─┘└─┴─┴─┴─┘└─┴─┴─┴─┘

Signature _____

Name (please print) _____

Address _____

City _____ State/Prov. _____ Zip/Postal Code _____

Telephone (Day) _____ (Evening) _____

Order online at www.cookbookresources.com — or

Mail to: Cookbook Resources   Call Toll Free: (866) 229-2665
       541 Doubletree Drive
       Highland Village, Texas 75077   Fax: (972) 317-6404